EDINBURGH FROM THE AIR
70 YEARS OF AERIAL PHOTOGRAPHY

BY THE SAME AUTHOR

Marchmont in Edinburgh 1984

Villages of Edinburgh Volume 1 (North) 1986

Villages of Edinburgh Volume 2 (South) 1987

Edinburgh: Sciennes and the Grange 1990

Yerbury: A Photographic Collection 1850–1993 1994

Edinburgh: Gorgie and Dalry 1995

Villages of Edinburgh: An Illustrated Guide Volume 1 (North) 1997

The District of Greenbank in Edinburgh 1998

Villages of Edinburgh: An Illustrated Guide Volume 2 (South) 1999

Old Tollcross, Morningside and Swanston 2001

Marchmont, Sciennes and the Grange 2001

Old Dalry in Edinburgh 2002

Old Gorgie 2002

Malcolm Cant

EDINBURGH FROM THE AIR

70 YEARS OF AERIAL PHOTOGRAPHY

MALCOLM CANT PUBLICATIONS IN ASSOCIATION WITH THE
ROYAL COMMISSION ON THE ANCIENT AND HISTORICAL MONUMENTS OF SCOTLAND

TO EVA AND IONA

MY TWIN GRANDDAUGHTERS IN AUSTRALIA

First published in 2003 by
Malcolm Cant Publications
13 Greenbank Row
Edinburgh EH10 5SY

Reprinted 2004

in association with the
Royal Commission on the Ancient and Historical Monuments of Scotland
John Sinclair House, 16 Bernard Terrace,
Edinburgh EH8 9NX

ISBN 0 9526099 6 7

British Library Cataloguing-in-Publication Data

A catalogue record for this book is available on request

Book and jacket designed by Mark Blackadder

Printed and bound in Spain by Book Print S.L.

Introduction and Acknowledgements

It has been quite a challenge, albeit an enjoyable one, to research and write *Edinburgh from the Air: 70 Years of Aerial Photography*, during which time I learned to see the City from a different angle. In recent years there has been a revival of interest in aerial photography throughout the country, due, in no small measure, to researchers and readers becoming more aware of the vast amount of material held by the Royal Commission on the Ancient and Historical Monuments of Scotland (RCAHMS) in the National Monuments Record of Scotland (NMRS). While researching my previous books on Edinburgh, I made frequent use of the NMRS photographic collections for pictures of buildings and street scenes, but I had not used the aerial photographs to any great extent. Some years ago I was fortunate to be shown a collection of glass plates of aerial views of Edinburgh, believed to have been taken in 1930, belonging to Edinburgh City Archives. The exact reason for the pictures being taken was not known but it was evident to me at the time that they were of great interest, especially when contrasted with modern views of the same locations. On enquiry to RCAHMS I was invited to extend my research into other decades rather than confine the idea to the narrower field of the 1930 pictures only. Looking back, I can say that that was when the idea of *Edinburgh from the Air: 70 Years of Aerial Photography* was born.

During 2000 I spent many productive hours selecting material in the RCAHMS library. I was frequently sidetracked and often ended up with many more images than could possibly be used in one book. The famous 'green boxes' which line the library shelves produced a large number of photographs, both colour and black and white, taken at intervals from the 1960s to the present day. Then David Easton of RCAHMS introduced me, in his characteristically enthusiastic way, to the Royal Air Force vertical and oblique aerial photographs of the 1940s and 1950s

held in NMRS. The 1940s photographs form the Scottish part of the National Survey of Britain undertaken by the Royal Air Force to assist the Ordnance Survey in their map revision during post-war years. When I reached that stage in my research I knew that we had a good selection of pictures from 1930 to the present day. All that needed to be done was to make a final selection and write the book. What could be simpler? The initial selection was almost three times more than was required but eventually the numbers were reduced to more manageable proportions, and the research began. Having completed earlier studies of various Edinburgh districts I was able to make good progress to begin with, but, when I came to areas of the city which were less well known to me, progress was much slower.

I was in some doubt as to whether to arrange the material in chronological or topographical order. Each method has its advantages and disadvantages. In the end I compromised and adopted a combination of the two methods. Each chapter deals with a geographical area (as illustrated on the map at the beginning of the book) and within each chapter the photographs are arranged chronologically. This has the advantage that readers will be able to find their 'side' of the town quickly, and then follow a chronological sequence showing how the area has changed over the years. The book is divided into three parts. Part One includes Chapter 1 (City Centre) and Chapter 2 (Inner Suburbs – such as Dalry, Marchmont and Abbeyhill). Part Two is the colour section and Part Three deals with the outlying parts of the City: Chapter 3, North; Chapter 4, South; Chapter 5, East; and Chapter 6, West. As oblique photographs of the City can often include a very wide area, there is some inevitable overlap between the chapters.

Each chapter opens with a double-page spread in colour and a list of the main districts included. The black and white sections of the book are laid out in a series of double-page spreads with the main aerial photograph alternating between a left-hand and right-hand page. A small vignette, with numbered references, has been included to assist readers in their understanding of the main picture. Each main aerial photograph is supported by descriptive text and either one or more 'land' pictures depicting a dominant part of the aerial view. As far as is practical, buildings and streets are named in the text as at the date of the photograph. The colour section consists of twenty full page illustrations taken between 1985 and 2002. These have been chosen: to illustrate some of the traditional Edinburgh views, such as Moray Place and the Crescents to the West End of Edinburgh; to show how the City's financial centre has moved southwards to include Lothian Road and Morrison Street; to demonstrate history in the making, for example, the Scottish Parliament under construction in Holyrood Road; and to show how parts of history have almost been lost to the casual observer, for example, the rig and furrow cultivation on Prestonfield Golf Course and the remains of a Second World War anti-aircraft gun battery at Liberton.

In putting this book together I have again relied on a great number of people for assistance on various topics. Publication of the book is a joint venture with the Royal Commission on the Ancient and Historical Monuments of Scotland whose staff have been involved in almost every aspect of the book. My particular thanks go to: Marilyn Brown; David Easton; Lesley Ferguson; Philip Graham; Kristina Johansson; Alan Leith; Ian Parker; Jack Stevenson; and collectively, the members of the Photographic Section. As already stated, most of the aerial photographs come from the NMRS collections and are Crown copyright: RCAHMS or Ministry of Defence, who have kindly given permission for reproduction. A small number (the 1930 aerial pictures) come from Edinburgh City Archives. For particular aspects of research I also thank: Broughton History Society; Edinburgh Academical Football Club; Edinburgh Airport Ltd; Edinburgh Room, Edinburgh Central Library; Edinburgh University, King's Buildings; Edinburgh University Library; Fettes College; George Heriot's School; Historic Scotland; Jenners; Museum of Flight; Napier University; Royal Botanic Garden Edinburgh; Royal Observatory; Royal Yacht *Britannia*; Saughton House; Standard Life Assurance Co.

In addition to the various libraries and institutions, several people provided information on individual photographs. They include: Jim Brennan; Mrs Betty Craig; Alan Duns; Dominic Gamble; John A. F. Gibb; Joanne Grant; D. Hunter; Mrs Peter Howard-Johnston; Charles McMaster; Mrs Frances Martin; Hamish Mearns; Mrs Sheila Miller; Phil and Jean Moffat; Sandy Mullay; Miss Jean Orr; Mrs Mary Profit; Ricky Raeburn; Jean Renwick; George Scammell; Sheila Skinner; George Staddon; Charles Terry; Joyce M. Wallace and Mae Watson. The names of those who lent photographs are included throughout the book.

After I had finished writing the book the serious business of publication began. Nicola Wood again edited the script to her usual high standard, Mark Blackadder creatively undertook page and cover design, Oula Jones completed a very comprehensive index, and Neville Moir dealt quickly and efficiently with all aspects of production. Without the commitment of these professional people I would not be able to publish my own books.

As always, I thank my wife Phyllis and the members of our extended family for their interest and assistance with numerous tasks.

MALCOLM CANT

Contents

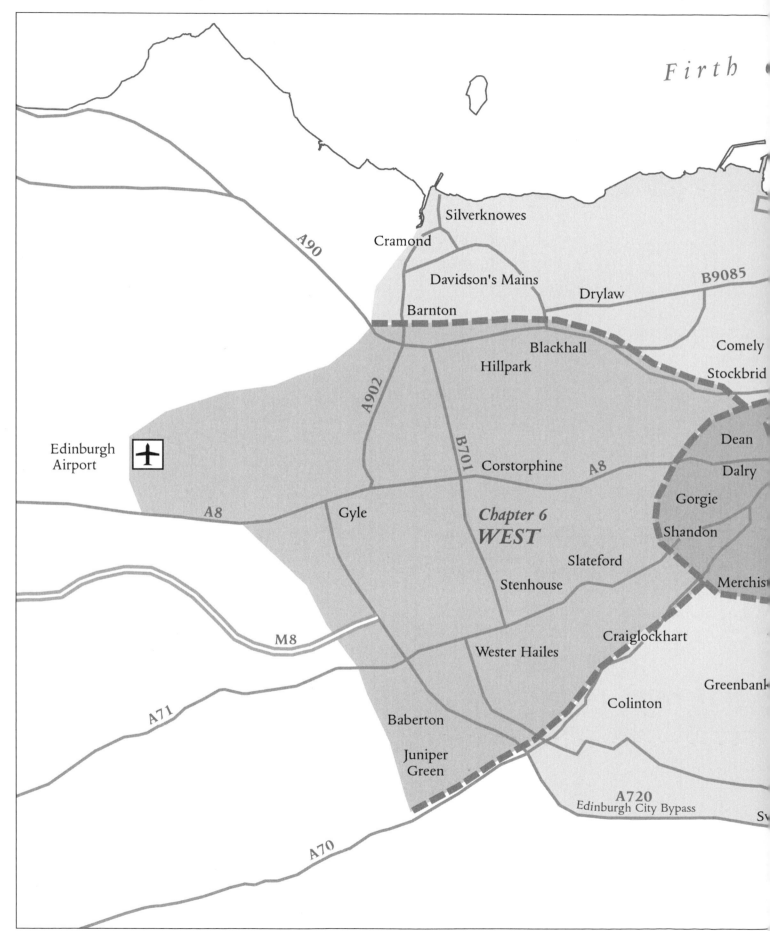

Firth

Silverknowes

Cramond

Davidson's Mains

Drylaw

B9085

Barnton

Blackhall

Comely

Hillpark

Stockbrid

A902

Dean

B701

Dalry

Edinburgh
Airport

Corstorphine

A8

Gorgie

A8

Gyle

Chapter 6
WEST

Shandon

Slateford

Merchis

Stenhouse

M8

Wester Hailes

Craiglockhart

Greenbank

Colinton

A71

Baberton

Juniper
Green

A70

A720
Edinburgh City Bypass

Sw

RCAHMS

ROYAL COMMISSION ON THE ANCIENT
AND HISTORICAL MONUMENTS OF SCOTLAND

The publisher acknowledges the assistance of the
Royal Commission on the Ancient and Historical Monuments of Scotland
in the production of this volume

Royal Commission on the Ancient and Historical Monuments of Scotland
John Sinclair House, 16 Bernard Terrace, Edinburgh, EH8 9NX

Telephone: +44 (0) 131 662 1456
Email: nmrs@rcahms.gov.uk
Website: www.rcahms.gov.uk

Many of the images included in this volume have been selected from the collections
of the National Monuments Record of Scotland (NMRS), the archive and database of
the Royal Commission on the Ancient and Historical Monuments of Scotland (RCAHMS).
RCAHMS records and interprets the sites, monuments and buildings of Scotland's past and
promotes a greater appreciation of their value through the NMRS, which is open to the
public from Monday to Friday 9.30am – 4.30pm. The RCAHMS website (www.rcahms.gov.uk)
gives access to CANMORE, the NMRS database, which contains information on
architectural, archaeological and maritime sites in Scotland, as well as details
of the collections held in the NMRS.

*Copies of RCAHMS photographs can be ordered directly from the address above,
quoting the reference number which appears near the photographs in the book*

PART ONE

Crown copyright: RCAHMS ref. D 56900 CN

City Centre

Edinburgh Castle during the Edinburgh
International Festival 1999. Behind the Castle,
clockwise, Saltire Court; Usher Hall;
Clydesdale Bank Plaza; Standard Life Assurance
Company; Caledonian Hotel; St John's Episcopal
Church; and St Cuthbert's Parish Church.

Fountainbridge, 1930

Two of the Old Town's ancient 'arterial' roads, Morrison Street on the left, and Fountainbridge on the right, converge at Main Point at the top of the picture. Stuart Harris, author of *The Place Names of Edinburgh*, suggests that Main Point may, in fact, refer to an early house or building rather than the road junction, and that *main*, being the Scots word for fine white bread, may provide a tantalising connection with Bread Street nearby.

One of the most interesting aspects of the picture is the vacant site at the top of Lothian Road which was used for the construction of Lothian House, the government tax office, in the early 1930s. The Art Deco building, now converted to residential accommodation, was designed by the architect, Stewart Kaye, with a low relief sculpture of a barge on its façade, commemorating the canal basin, Port Hopetoun, which occupied the site previously. In the bottom, left-hand corner of the picture is the distinctive curve of Gardner's Crescent, dating from 1822, which joins Morrison Street to Fountainbridge. Below the curved section of Gardner's Crescent is the square formation of Rosebank Buildings, 1859, and the slightly earlier Rosebank Cottages, 1853, nearer to the Caledonian railway line

as it runs under Morrison Street.

On the extreme right, three small boats are moored at the truncated Union Canal which at one time continued through Fountainbridge to Port Hamilton and Port Hopetoun. Careful comparison of the street layout with the pre-1930 photograph below shows the buildings which have been erected after the canal was shortened. When the Union Canal crossed Fountainbridge, vehicle traffic was carried on an iron bridge which was later resited over the canal in Leamington Terrace. In 2002 the bridge was renovated and the lifting mechanism repaired. Finally, the T-shaped Tollcross School, dating from 1911, is in the top right-hand corner.

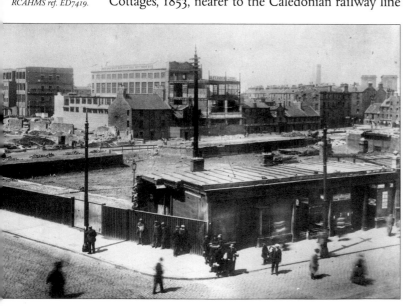

EDINBURGH from the Air.

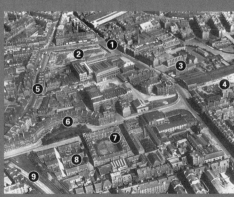

1. Fountainbridge
2. Port Hopetoun
3. Tollcross School
4. Boats
5. Morrison Street
6. Gardner's Crescent
7. Rosebank Buildings
8. Rosebank Cottages
9. Railway

1. Royal High School
2. National Monument
3. Nelson Column
4. Bridewell
5. City Observatory
6. Site of Calton Jail
7. Stewart Monument

Calton Hill and Regent Road, 1930

Calton Hill has been photographed many times over the years but this picture is particularly significant as it shows, on the extreme right, the site of Calton Jail and the Bridewell, partially cleared for the construction of St Andrew's House built between 1936 and 1939. It was built to designs by Thomas S. Tait to accommodate the Scottish Office. Previously, the site was occupied by the Bridewell, nearer to the Royal High School building, and Calton Jail nearer to the East End.

The Bridewell, Edinburgh's 'House of Correction', was designed by Robert Adam and the foundation stone was laid by the Earl of Morton on 30 November 1791. In the photograph, most of the building is still standing but the substantial gatehouse and boundary walls have been removed. The light-coloured area of ground (nearer to the East End) contained Calton Jail, its small windows, high perimeter walls and impregnable gatehouse creating an equally forebidding appearance. Its foundation stone was laid in September 1815 after several other sites, including the south side of Princes Street, had been considered but rejected.

By contrast, the principal monuments on Calton Hill remain largely unaltered. Only twelve pillars were erected of the National Monument to those who fell in the Napoleonic Wars. The intended copy of the Parthenon by C. R. Cockerell and William H. Playfair, which would have greatly enhanced Edinburgh's claim to be the Athens of the North, was halted in 1829 when the appeal money ran out. To the right of the National Monument, the Nelson Column was designed in 1807 by Robert Burn with commanding views over the city, but getting a rear view only of Thomas Hamilton's Grecian masterpiece, the Royal High School, when it was erected between 1825 and 1829. The square enclosure, also on the summit of Calton Hill, contains: the cross-shaped City Observatory, 1818; Observatory House, 1776, on the south-west corner of the boundary wall; and the Professor John Playfair Monument on the south-east corner, designed by his nephew, the architect, William H. Playfair. Outside the enclosure, on the right, is the monument to the great philosopher, Dugald Stewart, and further down Regent Road, a similar circular colonnade to Robert Burns.

Below left. Some of the men who built the extension to Calton Jail between 1882 and 1884. *Courtesy of Hamish Mearns.*

Above. Calton Jail is the most dominant building in the centre of the picture as viewed from Calton Hill. When the jail was constructed in 1815 it took the inmates from the Old Tolbooth, and when it was demolished in the mid-1920s its inmates were transferred to Saughton Prison, designed by HM Office of Works in 1925. Part of the Bridewell roof and gatehouse can also be seen on the left of the photograph. *Courtesy of the author.*

Dean Cemetery and the Art Galleries, 1930

Courtesy of Edinburgh City Archives

Dean Cemetery, in the top left-hand corner of the photograph, was laid out in 1845 on the site of the former Dean House, home of William Nisbet of Dean, Lord Provost of Edinburgh on two occasions in the early seventeenth century. Dean House was completely demolished but stones from it were incorporated in the cemetery wall and also in various buildings in Dean village nearby. Painted ceiling panels from the house were also saved and are now on display in the new Museum of Scotland in Chambers Street.

The photograph is dominated by two buildings on either side of Belford Road which are now art galleries: the Paolozzi Gallery is adjacent to Dean Cemetery and the Scottish National Gallery of Modern Art stands in its own grounds in the centre of the picture. The first building, with the twin square towers, now used as the Paolozzi Gallery, was built as the Dean Orphan Hospital between 1831 and 1833 to plans by the architect, Thomas Hamilton. After a variety of later uses, including the Dean Education Centre, the building was converted in the late 1990s to an art gallery, principally to house the works of the Leith-born sculptor, Eduardo Paolozzi.

The building now occupied as the Gallery of Modern Art was built as John Watson's School, designed in 1828 by the architect, William Burn, as a school for the maintenance and education of destitute children. It was converted to be the new home of the Scottish National Gallery of Modern Art and opened on 14 August 1984.

At the top of the picture, Belford Road crosses the Water of Leith at Belford Bridge, opened on 22 July 1887 by the Rt Hon. Sir Thomas Clark, Lord Provost of Edinburgh. The engineers were Cunningham Blyth & Westland, and the contractors were Henderson Matthew & Co. It was built to replace an earlier bridge on the same site.

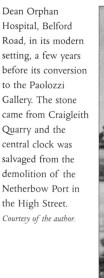

Dean Orphan Hospital, Belford Road, in its modern setting, a few years before its conversion to the Paolozzi Gallery. The stone came from Craigleith Quarry and the central clock was salvaged from the demolition of the Netherbow Port in the High Street. *Courtesy of the author.*

1. Dean Cemetery
2. Dean Orphan Hospital
3. Belford Road
4. John Watson's School
5. Belford Bridge

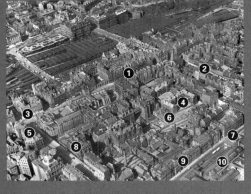

1. High Street
2. South Bridge
3. Matthew & Son Ltd
4. Tron Square
5. Melbourne Place
6. Argyle Brewery
7. Chambers Street
8. Old Sheriff Court
9. Heriot-Watt College
10. Royal Scottish Museum

George IV Bridge, 1930

The Royal Mile runs diagonally from the left-hand side of the photograph to the top right-hand corner. The rectangle bounded by the High Street, South Bridge, Chambers Street and George IV Bridge contains a conglomeration of buildings, some of which have been demolished or greatly altered since this photograph was taken in 1930. Although individual buildings have been lost, the basic street layout remains intact.

The short section of the Lawnmarket between Bank Street and St Giles Street is occupied by James Matthew & Son Ltd, drapers, clothiers, and linoleum and carpet retailers, whose extensive premises also occupied adjacent buildings in Bank Street and St Giles Street. The whole block was demolished for the construction of a new Sheriff Court House in 1934. Melbourne Place (the north-west section of George IV Bridge) was home to Alex Ferguson Ltd, Confectioners, makers of the famous Edinburgh Rock. The building, and the corner section of Victoria Terrace, were demolished in 1966 and replaced by the headquarters of what was then Lothian Regional Council. Also on George IV Bridge, on the site of the present National Library of Scotland, is an earlier Sheriff Court House which was in use prior to 1934.

In the bottom right-hand corner of the picture, only the roof lights of the Royal Scottish Museum appear. The other side of Chambers Street, however, shows Heriot-Watt College, now relocated at Riccarton as Heriot-Watt University. To the left, the high chimney stack and the surrounding buildings were demolished for an extension to the College. The south-facing Tron Square, to the left of South Bridge, provides an ideal spot for washing lines slung across the courtyard between the iron balconies. Between Tron Square and Heriot-Watt College is the square chimney of the Argyle Brewery, dating from 1710, run by Campbell, Hope & King Ltd. Part of it survives as Taylor's Hall in the Cowgate.

Further afield is the huge expanse of Waverley Station, the ornamental garden on the roof of Waverley Market, the North British Hotel (now the Balmoral) and various buildings at the east end of Princes Street.

Above. Edinburgh Sheriff Court House which stood on George IV Bridge before being demolished for the construction of the National Library of Scotland.
Courtesy of the author.

Left. This derelict doorway, leading to Campbell, Hope and King's Argyle Brewery, still had the inscription 'Entry to Brewery Counting Room' in 1990, shortly before most of the building was demolished. The metal plate above the doorway masks the Royal Coat of Arms.
Courtesy of the author.

George IV Bridge, 1951

This 1951 photograph shows part of the area seen in the previous 1930 view. The premises of James Matthew & Son Ltd, in the Lawnmarket, has been demolished and replaced by the new Sheriff Court House. In Melbourne Place, Ferguson's premises for making Edinburgh Rock are intact, but the most interesting aspect is the girder work for the National Library of Scotland, seen in the bottom left-hand corner of the picture.

The National Library of Scotland is a direct descendant of the Advocates' Library which was inaugurated in 1689. From 1710 the Advocates' Library enjoyed the privilege of legal deposit, thus elevating it to the status of a national library, in practice, if not in name. In the 1920s, Sir Alexander Grant gifted a total of £200,000 to establish a National Library and provide for it a completely new building. The National Library of Scotland was created by Act of Parliament in 1925 when the Advocates' Library gifted its substantial collection of books to the nation, retaining only the law library for its own use. Plans for a new building were drawn up using the site on George IV Bridge. Although construction of the new library building, designed by Reginald Fairlie & Partners, began in 1938, it was delayed by the Second World War and was not opened until 1956. The photograph, taken in 1951, shows the girder work only which was erected before the outbreak of war. The stonework and joiner work was completed later by Colin Macandrew & Partners Ltd, of West End Place, off Dalry Road. The firm was established by Colin Macandrew in 1882 and went on to complete many public buildings in Edinburgh and throughout Scotland, including Morningside High Church, the Royal Bank of Scotland in Hope Street, King's Buildings and Redford Barracks.

Opposite the National Library is the Edinburgh Central Public Library, designed by George Washington Browne, and opened in 1890.

The church building on the left, Tolbooth St John's, was built 1839–44 to designs by James Gillespie Graham and A. W. N. Pugin. It was completely redesigned internally in the late 1990s as The Hub, the headquarters of the Edinburgh International Festival. To the right of the Tolbooth St John's are the towers of New College and the Assembly Hall (at present the temporary home of the Scottish Parliament) designed by William H. Playfair and built between 1845 and 1850.

Part of the steelwork only had been erected when this photograph of the National Library of Scotland was taken in the early 1950s. It also shows some of the individual arches of George IV Bridge, designed by Thomas Hamilton and built between 1829 and 1834. It was named after George IV who visited Edinburgh in 1822. The building of George IV Bridge created a new south approach to the City, envisaged by the 1827 Improvement Act. When completed, the Bridge was built up on both sides leaving only two arches visible – one crossing the Cowgate, and the other, further south, crossing Merchant Street. The Edinburgh Central Public Library is also in the picture, behind the bus.

Courtesy of the former directors of Colin Macandrew & Partners Ltd.

1. Tolbooth St John's
2. New College and Assembly Hall
3. Central Library
4. Melbourne Place
5. Sheriff Court
6. National Library under construction

1. St Stephen's Church
2. Eyre Crescent
3. Davidson Church
4. Memorial Park
5. Heriot Hill House

Eyre Crescent, 1951

Eyre Crescent, in the centre of the picture, was built in the early 1890s, almost encircling Davidson Church designed by John Starforth in 1879. The halls to the rear of the church, although following Starforth's ideas, were designed by George Washington Browne a decade later. The church was opened on 6 April 1881 by a United Presbyterian congregation which had previously worshipped at Queen Street Hall. After Davidson Church formed a union with St Bernard's in 1945, the Eyre Crescent building was surplus to requirements and later became a warehouse, before being demolished, c. 1989.

The tall clock tower of St Stephen's Church is shrouded in the smoke of countless chimneys. The church was designed by William H. Playfair and opened in 1828, but by the mid-1950s a grand scheme to divide the church horizontally was already under way. A new concrete floor was inserted at what had previously been the gallery level, considerably reducing the size of the auditorium. This had the welcome effect of reducing the costly heating bills and improving the acoustics, which at least one preacher had described as 'like shouting in a quarry'.

To the left of Eyre Crescent, the industrial units entered from Eyre Terrace included Patriothall Laundry Ltd, and J. T. Hislop & Son, Motor Engineers. The open ground nearby is King George V Memorial Park, home to St Bernard's Football Club up until 1942. A small stand at the south end of the pitch, near Royal Crescent, appears to have been removed by the time this photograph was taken on 7 December 1951. The junction of Rodney Street and Broughton Road is in the bottom left-hand corner of the picture. The circular driveway with the central flagpole relates to Heriot Hill House dating from 1788, later used as a Royal Navy and Royal Marine Club.

By 1989 when this photograph was taken, Davidson Church in Eyre Crescent had been demolished and the site cleared.

Crown copyright: RCAHMS ref. B/21759.

East End and St James' Square, 1951

The principal buildings in the centre of the picture are Register House, New Register House, Royal Bank of Scotland Headquarters, National Bank of Scotland Headquarters (now part of Royal Bank), with the North British Hotel (now the Balmoral) on the left. Further afield, and rising above the height of the surrounding buildings are: the spire of St Andrew's Church (now St Andrew's and St George's) in George Street; the Melville Monument (to Visc. Melville, Treasurer to the Navy) in the centre of St Andrew Square; and St Stephen's Church in Stockbridge.

Register House at the east end of Princes Street, begun in 1774, was designed by Robert Adam to house Scotland's public records. The stone came from Craigleith and Hailes quarries but it took many years to complete and there were frequent revisions in costs. To the north-west, New Register House was built between 1858 and 1863 to hold additional records following the compulsory registration of births, deaths and marriages in 1855. Its Italianate style, by the architect, Robert Matheson, contrasts well with Robert Adam's adjacent work. The huge clock tower of the North British Hotel is on the left of the picture. The hotel, by W. Hamilton Beattie, who also designed Jenner's in Princes Street, was opened in 1902 with 700 rooms (over 300 of which were bedrooms) and required 13,000 tons of stone for its construction.

In St Andrew Square, the bulky, light-coloured building on the corner of Meuse Lane is the head office of the National Bank of Scotland (now part of the Royal Bank) and to the right, the Royal's own head office sits back from the main building line. When this photograph was taken in 1951 St Andrew Square was still being used as a bus 'station'. The eighteenth-century St James' Square lying to the right of Register House was demolished in 1965, along with the top part of Leith Street, to make way for the St James Centre.

Below right. In the early 1950s this is what the East End of Edinburgh looked like before the construction of the St James Centre. Register House is on the left and Francis Petrie, Wholesale Tobacconists, is at No. 3 Leith Street Terrace which provided a pedestrian walkway above the level of Leith Street. Part of St James' Square shows in the gap. Courtesy of Duncan McMillan

Above. The men who planned and built Woolworth's Stores at the east end of Princes Street pose for the camera on Thursday 18 February 1926. The store was extended to the west in 1956 and closed in 1984. *Courtesy of the author.*

1. St Stephen's Church
2. St Andrew's Church
3. Melville Monument
4. National Bank
5. Royal Bank
6. New Register House
7. North British Hotel
8. Register House
9. St James' Square

1. St Cuthbert's Parish Church
2. Caledonian Hotel
3. St John's Episcopal Church
4. Charlotte Square
5. George Street

West End, 1951

This unusual photograph of the West End was taken, looking south-west, from a point high above the west end of George Street on Friday, 7 December 1951. Before the days of parking restrictions, cars are lining most kerbsides, with end-on parking in George Street and parts of Charlotte Square.

The most dominant building in the centre of the picture is the Caledonian Hotel. The left-hand entrance led to the hotel and the right-hand one to the railway station. The tracks, and the pitched roofs of the station, can be seen behind the hotel. When the Caledonian Railway first laid its track into the centre of Edinburgh in 1848 the rail terminus was further up Lothian Road nearer to the present-day West Approach Road. A very rudimentary station was built on the West End site in 1870 but was replaced by a much grander structure in 1894. In 1903, the 1894 station building was incorporated into the Caledonian Hotel, designed by J. M. Dick Peddie and George Washington Browne.

Equally attractive, but of much smaller scale, is St John's Episcopal Church on the corner of Princes Street and Lothian Road. It was designed around 1815 by William Burn and cost £18,000 to build. To its left is St Cuthbert's Parish Church in the hollow. There has been some form of ecclesiastical presence here since the twelfth century but in 1894, after several attempts at saving the medieval church, Hippolyte Blanc, the famous church architect, undertook a rebuild incorporating the steeple of 1789.

Charlotte Square is in the bottom right-hand corner. It is generally accepted as the jewel in the crown of Edinburgh's New Town. Designed by Robert Adam, the square was begun in the early 1790s but was not completed until about 1811. A short section of the south side of George Street is also visible in the picture. In 1951 George Street was the hub of Edinburgh's business community with many banks, insurance offices and building societies. The south corner of George Street and Charlotte Square is occupied by the Ocean, Accident & Guarantee Corporation Ltd, whose windows were emblazoned with all manner of portentous slogans: Fire; Life; Burglary; Accident; Liability; Sickness and Disease.

In the early 1950s, Edinburgh's public transport was still dominated by the electric tram system. As is evident in the foreground, the track and supporting setts were in constant need of repair. On the left of the picture a group of south-bound commuters are huddled onto one of the tram stop islands, but most of the trams are going in the opposite direction.
Courtesy of Duncan McMillan.

Rutland Square, 1951

This picture was taken, on the same day, in the opposite direction to the previous view of the West End, this time looking north-east across Rutland Square and Street. The pitched roofs of the Caledonian Station, latterly referred to as Princes Street Station, lie to the right of the Square. Rutland Square and Street date from around 1830, earlier than even the first Caledonian Station building, erected in 1848 further up Lothian Road. When the Caledonian Railway built another station building in 1870, a large section of the south side of Rutland Street was demolished to accommodate it. Only the roofs of Rutland Place are visible in the photograph, the former church building having a frontage to the Place and the Street.

The clock and campanile of St George's West Church (originally a Free Church) are on the extreme left of the picture on the corner of Stafford Street and Shandwick Place. The body of the church was designed by David Bryce in 1866 but the tower, by R. Rowand Anderson, was not completed until 1881. Opposite the church are the first few terraced houses of Atholl Crescent, begun in 1825. When this photograph was taken, however, many of the houses had been acquired by the Edinburgh College of Domestic Science often referred to simply as 'Atholl Crescent'. The College was founded as the Edinburgh School of Cookery in 1875 in Chambers Street, and, after several other moves, came to Atholl Crescent in 1891 where they remained until 1970. The College is now incorporated into Queen Margaret University College at Clerwood.

Right. Princes Street Station, 1965, in the days of steam, looking west towards the bridge, beyond the station, which carried Morrison Street across the main track. The tenement behind the signal box still remains, immediately opposite the present-day Edinburgh International Conference Centre.
Photograph by David Easton.

Right. The basic layout of the streets around the West End has not changed greatly in this 1988 view but the railway lines have been removed and replaced by a car park. An extension to the Caledonian Hotel and part of the new financial district are now built on the site.
Crown copyright: RCAHMS ref. A/55897.

1. St George's West Church
2. Rutland Place
3. Rutland Street
4. Caledonian Railway Station
5. Atholl Crescent
6. Rutland Square

1. Edinburgh University
2. St Patrick's RC Church
3. Empire Theatre
4. Lady Glenorchy's Church
5. Nicolson Square
6. Nicolson Street

Nicolson Street, 1951

The main thoroughfare is Nicolson Street, with Nicolson Square on the left, looking north to the dome of Edinburgh University's Old Quad on South Bridge. The University has had a strong presence in the area for well over 200 years. The outer façade of the quadrangle was designed by Robert Adam in 1789, and the inner elevations by William H. Playfair in 1819, who also did much of the interior. The dome was not completed until 1887 following a generous bequest by Robert Cox WS, of Gorgie. In a light-hearted reference to the Cox family's successful business as glue manufacturers, it was always said that the dome of Edinburgh University would never have been completed had it not been for Cox's glue. More information and a photograph of Cox's Glue Works appear on pages 40–41.

Mid-way between the University dome and Nicolson Square, the much smaller dome is the Empire Theatre. The earliest theatrical building on the site was the Dunedin Hall, dating from 1830, followed by the Royal Amphitheatre, Alhambra Music Hall, Queen's Theatre and Newsome's Circus. In 1892 the site was completely redeveloped as the Empire Palace Theatre, designed by the theatre architect, Frank Matcham. Unfortunately, the building sustained serious fire damage on 9 May 1911 when an act went wrong involving the great illusionist, Lafayette. The safety curtain protected the audience but Lafayette and several other people perished in the blaze. The damage was repaired fairly quickly but in 1927 the Milburn brothers were employed to redesign and rebuild much of the old theatre which was opened again on 1 October 1928. After being used as a bingo hall from 1963 until 1991, the Empire was completely revamped and refronted and opened as the Edinburgh Festival Theatre in 1994.

On the extreme right of the picture, there are two ecclesiastical buildings with very different origins: Lady Glenorchy's Church, built between 1909 and 1913 on the site of a much earlier chapel, is in Roxburgh Place; and St Patrick's Roman Catholic Church is in the Cowgate. The St Patrick's building started as an Episcopalian chapel in the late eighteenth century, but was redesigned internally when the building was bought by the Roman Catholic Church in 1856.

The auditorium of the Empire Palace Theatre in Nicolson Street, probably around 1910, shortly before the serious fire of 1911.
Crown copyright: RCAHMS ref. ED/11650.

Bristo, 1966

Crown copyright. MoD ref. 28/BAF/5210 0028

Near the centre of the photograph, the light-coloured disc is the copper dome of the Usher Hall. To the right, the old Poole's Synod Hall in Castle Terrace appears to be in the throes of demolition, creating one of Edinburgh's notorious 'holes in the ground', not filled until Saltire Court was built on the site. Behind the Usher Hall are the pitched roofs of Princes Street Railway Station. Edinburgh Castle has scaffolding anchored to the rock above Johnston Terrace and the esplanade is occupied by the raised seating for the Edinburgh Military Tattoo.

To the left of the Castle, the Tollcross and Lauriston areas have several buildings which have not stood the test of time. The square, concrete-slab structure of Lauriston House, 1960, once the offices of the National Coal Board, was demolished in 2002 after remaining empty for several years. The more elegant building owned by Goldberg's Stores, also dating from 1960, was demolished for the construction of housing in High Riggs. Both buildings appear in more detail on pages 62-63. Heriot's School stands in its own grounds on the north side of Lauriston Place. Work on the building began in 1628 under the direction of William Wallace, Master Mason to the Crown, but was not completed until 1650.

Two very contrasting sites are in the bottom left-hand quarter of the picture. The shallow-domed McEwan Hall, designed by R. Rowand Anderson, was begun in 1888 shortly after completion of the adjacent Medical School by the same architect. The overall effect in Teviot Place would have been even more impressive had the intended campanile been completed at the east end of the Medical School. The tall featureless building, near the corner of the picture, is Edinburgh University's Appleton Tower built in the mid-1960s. Much of the area to the right of the Appleton Tower was demolished shortly after this photograph was taken to accommodate a new road system, which, even now, is not remotely in harmony with its surroundings.

1. Princes Street Station
2. Usher Hall
3. Synod Hall
4. Goldberg's Store
5. Lauriston House
6. Heriot's School
7. McEwan Hall
8. Appleton Tower
9. Bristo Street
10. Potterrow

1. Edinburgh & Granton Railway
2. New Club
3. Site of NB & M
4. Bank of Scotland
5. Site of LRC
6. George IV Bridge

Old and New Towns, 1966

Aerial photography is ideal for highlighting the fundamental difference between the tightly packed buildings of the Old Town, at the bottom of the picture, and the disciplined parallelograms of the New Town in the middle distance. The 1960s were a difficult time for conservationists in Edinburgh, faced, as they were, with the concept of knock it down and start again. The damage inflicted was serious but could have been much worse.

The line of George IV Bridge runs, almost vertically, from the bottom edge of the picture, in the direction of the Head Office of the Bank of Scotland. The bank was built between 1802 and 1806 but did not take on its present-day appearance until after David Bryce's remodelling of 1863. On the far left, the old bench-style seating for the Military Tattoo rises high above the esplanade, and in the bottom left-hand corner, pupils can be seen at the rear of Heriot's School. The demolition men, however, are already at work clearing a space for Lothian Regional Council's headquarters on the west corner of George IV Bridge (Melbourne Place) and Lawnmarket. More destruction, with even less justification, is evident on Princes Street with the removal of the North British & Mercantile Insurance building, creating a gap site to be filled later by British Home Stores. A few yards west of the junction with Hanover Street, two other buildings, blackened by decades of smoke, await their fate – the New Club and the Life Association of Scotland. On the right of the picture is the roof garden of the original Waverley Market, most of which was demolished in 1974. The resultant 'hole in the ground' was not redeveloped as a shopping mall until a decade later.

Stockbridge, Canonmills, the playing fields of Warriston and Goldenacre (on the east side of Inverleith Row) and the railway line from Heriot Hill goods station to Granton are all at the top of the photograph.

The demolition of Melbourne Place, between Victoria Terrace and the Lawnmarket, took place in 1966 for the construction of the headquarters of Lothian Regional Council. The site was previously occupied mainly by Alex Ferguson Ltd, Confectioners, who manufactured Edinburgh Rock. The buildings at the back are Liddell's Court and other tenements, Nos. 298–320 Lawnmarket.

Crown copyright: RCAHMS ref. ED/2159.

New Town, 1984

The geometric patterns formed by the principal streets of Edinburgh's New Town are in stark contrast to the narrow wynds and closes of the Old Town. The original intention was to make George Street the principal thoroughfare, connecting with St Andrew Square at the east end and Charlotte Square at the west end. As it turned out, Princes Street became more dominant as a result of its once-famous retail establishments, but at the present day it is desperately seeking a new image. By contrast, George Street appears to have moved effortlessly from being almost exclusively commercial to absorb an interesting mixture of new retail outlets, bars and restaurants. Edinburgh's latest traffic management scheme has ensured that Queen Street has everything that a racetrack needs, except the pits, chicanes and gravel traps.

Edinburgh's Old Town was grossly overcrowded when 'The Proposals for carrying on certain Public Works in the city of Edinburgh' were published in 1752. Part of the proposals, enthusiastically championed by Sir George Drummond, Lord Provost of Edinburgh on six occasions between 1725 and 1764, was to expand the city to the north and create a New Town with wide streets, squares and crescents. The resulting architectural competition was won by James Craig, a young and apparently arrogant architect with little previous form. One of his earliest brushes with the Town Council was over his decision to use the name St Giles Street for the south-most thoroughfare which was quickly renamed Princes Street. The Town's objection to the name St Giles Street appears to have been based on the rather unsavoury reputation of St Giles Street in London. Both Princes Street and Queen Street were always intended to have buildings on one side only to take full advantage of the excellent views of the Castle to the south and the Firth of Forth to the north. Even after the first North Bridge was opened to traffic in 1772 (after a serious partial collapse in 1769), and the introduction of financial inducements to build in the New Town, progress was slow. By about 1781 St Andrew Square was more or less completed; by 1790 Princes Street, George Street and Queen Street had reached as far west as Hanover Street; but Charlotte Square (first named St George's Square) was not finished until 1820. In 1831 Edinburgh's population was 136,000, almost double what it had been thirty years before, boosted, no doubt, by the huge amount of new development which had taken place.

Left. On Friday, 7 December 1951 when this photograph was taken of George Street, meters and other parking restrictions have not yet been introduced but there is almost continuous end-on parking on both sides of the street. The centre of the road is still occupied by tram tracks.
Crown copyright: MoD ref. 58/813 PFFO, 385.

Right. This undated image of George Street obviously belongs to a more leisurely age with a few carriages waiting at the strategically placed stepping on blocks at the kerbside. The photograph is taken looking east at the junction with Hanover Street. The statue of George IV is in the centre of the junction and St Andrew's Church, opened in 1784, (now St Andrew's and St George's) is on the north side of the street.
Courtesy of the author.

1. St Andrew Square
2. Queen Street
3. George Street
4. Princes Street

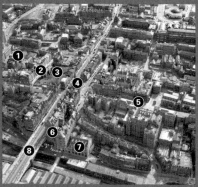

1. St Patrick's RC Church
2. Earl of Morton's House
3. Site of Scandic Hotel
4. Tron Kirk
5. High Street
6. Scotsman
7. City Art Centre
8. North Bridge

High Street and the Bridges, 1983

Left of centre is the Tron Kirk at the junction of North Bridge, South Bridge and the High Street. The Tron Kirk was built by John Mylne Jun. between 1636 and 1647 but was extensively remodelled in 1785. It has not had a congregation since Sunday 28 September 1952 when the minister and congregation moved to a new church, Tron-Moredun, in Craigour Gardens. The Tron Kirk took its name from 'the tron' or burgh weighbeam which stood at the head of Blair Street. At the present day the Kirk has been gutted internally to reveal the foundations and part of the walls of the sixteenth-century Marlin's Wynd.

To the left of the Tron Kirk, the tall building, erected in 1870, with the light-coloured roof is a branch of the Bank of Scotland, now, appropriately, the Bank Hotel. To the left again, most of the ground between Niddry Street and Blackfriars Street was cleared many years ago and lay undeveloped until 1990 when the Scandic Hotel (now the Holiday and Crowne Plaza), designed by Ian Begg Architects, was built. The surviving building on the extreme left of the vacant site is the Earl of Morton's House dating from the sixteenth century.

Another important Old Town church is St Patrick's Roman Catholic sitting back from the street line of the Cowgate. It was built in 1792 as an Episcopal chapel and bought by the Roman Catholic church in 1856.

The first North Bridge spanned the valley between the Old Town and the New Town in 1772, but was replaced in 1897 by the bridge seen in the photograph. The ornate building on the east side of the bridge is the Carlton Highland Hotel, part of which was previously occupied by Patrick Thomson's Cash Drapery Stores. On the west side are the headquarters of *The Scotsman* newspaper which were moved to new premises in Holyrood Road in 1999. The newspaper was once published in a much smaller office in Cockburn Street nearby. When Scotsman Publications moved out of the North Bridge premises, the building was renovated as the Scotsman Hotel, retaining and enhancing most of the original architectural features. In Market Street the five-storey building with the attic windows to the right of *The Scotsman* building is the City Art Centre, converted in 1979 from premises owned by C. R. McRitchie & Co. Ltd, Wholesale Hosiery Merchants. The Centre has attracted several world-renowned exhibitions, notably *The Gold of the Pharaohs* in 1988.

St Giles' Cathedral and the City Chambers, on the right of the picture, appear in the following photographs.

From a more elegant age, an advertisement for Patrick Thomson Ltd, Cash Drapery Stores, which were on the east side of North Bridge, partly in the building now occupied as the Carlton Highland Hotel.

Courtesy of the author.

The upper part of the picture shows the extensive glass-roofed area of the Waverley Station. In the 1840s there were three train companies using Waverley Station, namely, the North British Railway, the Edinburgh & Glasgow Railway, and the Edinburgh, Perth & Dundee Railway. After the North British absorbed the other two companies, it held a competition to design a completely new station. The competition was won by Charles Jopp and the station was built between 1868 and 1874.

The quadrangle in the centre of the picture is the City Chambers. In the middle of the eighteenth century the site was occupied by several old tene-

The Thistle Chapel, at the south-east corner of St Giles' Cathedral, was designed by Sir Robert Lorimer and opened on 19 July 1910.
Courtesy of the author.

ments, notably Mary King's Close infamously afflicted by plague in 1645, inhabited for a further 250 years and now a visitor attraction. Following an Act of Parliament in 1753 most of the ground was cleared and the foundation stone was laid on 13 September 1753 for a Customs House and Exchange, the latter intended as a meeting place for the City's merchants. Previously, the merchants still preferred to conduct their business in the open, often around the base of the statue of Charles II in Parliament Square. When the building was completed in 1761 only one public office was located there, namely the Custom House, the remainder being used as the Exchange. However, in 1809 when the Custom House became vacant the Town Council occupied it and on 14 May 1811 the building became known as the City Chambers. By the end of the nineteenth century the entire building was under municipal control.

The photograph also provides an unusual view of St Giles' Cathedral, its light-coloured roof contrasting with the darker crown spire and finials. There has been a church on the site since at least 1130, its great antiquity alluded to by A. Ian Dunlop in *The Kirks of Edinburgh*: 'Its crowned steeple stands over a church which, albeit changed in outward and inward appearance again and again, has witnessed great national events through the centuries and been used, for worship, by Roman Catholic, Episcopalian, Presbyterian, by General Assembly, Lord High Commissioner, by nobility and Sovereign, and always by ordinary Christian people'.

The Law Courts are in the bottom left-hand corner of the picture. The Signet Library and the Advocates' Library are on the left, both of which communicate with Parliament House. To the right of Parliament House are the Inner and Outer Houses of the Court of Session. The Court of Session, as the supreme civil court in Scotland, was established in 1532 by James V.

1. Waverley Station
2. City Chambers
3. Mercat Cross
4. St Giles' Cathedral
5. Law Courts
6. Parliament House

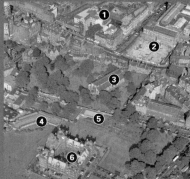

1. New Sheriff Court
2. Site of New Museum of Scotland
3. Greyfriars Kirk
4. Greyfriars Building
5. Nursery
6. Heriot's School

Heriot's School and Greyfriars Kirk, 1994

Greyfriars Kirk, surrounded by its ancient graveyard, is in the centre of the picture. It took its present name, Greyfriars, Tolbooth and Highland, on 28 February 1979, on the union of the congregations of Greyfriars Kirk and Highland Tolbooth St John's who previously worshipped in the Lawnmarket building now occupied as The Hub, the headquarters of the Edinburgh International Festival. Greyfriars burial ground is older than the church itself. Mary, Queen of Scots gave the ground to the City in 1562 to create a new burial ground as the space beside St Giles' Cathedral was full up. In 1601 Greyfriars was chosen as the site of a new church, the first to be built in Edinburgh since the Reformation of 1560. The first Greyfriars Kirk was begun in 1611 and the church was opened in 1620. Over the years Greyfriars has been rebuilt and altered on several occasions and has featured in several important historical events, notably the National Covenant in 1638, signed (in their own blood) by those opposed to Charles I's decree imposing Episcopal rule on Scotland. One of the most visited monuments in the burial ground is the Martyrs' Prison, although, contrary to popular belief, the Covenanters were not, in fact, imprisoned here but on a piece of land, near Forrest Hill, off Forrest Road, now built over.

The quadrangle at the bottom of the photograph is George Heriot's Hospital, now a co-educational primary and secondary school. Work on the building was started in 1628 by William Wallace, Master Mason to the Crown, but it was not finished until about 1650. The money to build it came from George Heriot, royal goldsmith and banker, who left the sum of nearly £24,000 to build a charity school for the upbringing and education of 'puire fatherless bairnes, friemens sones of that Toune of Edinburgh'. Owing to various delays in the building work, the first boys were not admitted until 1659. More recent additions, also seen in the picture, are the angle-shaped Greyfriars Building, the first phase of which was opened in 1983, and the Nursery, opened in 1992.

In the top right-hand corner of the photograph, preliminary concrete work only has been done for the lower floors of the Museum of Scotland, built in 1998 on the corner of Chambers Street and George IV Bridge.

The new Museum of Scotland, photographed in 1999, is in the centre of the picture at the corner of Chambers Street and George IV Bridge. It was designed by Benson & Forsyth of Edinburgh and opened on 29 November 1998 by HRH Queen Elizabeth II. *Crown copyright: RCAHMS ref. D/56531.*

Holyrood, 1994

The Palace of Holyroodhouse, and the older, ruined Holyrood Abbey (to the left of the Palace) are in the centre of the picture. Over a period of almost a thousand years Holyrood has changed its use on numerous occasions to include monastery, Scottish Parliament, parish church, royal residence and leading tourist attraction. The Abbey was founded in 1128 by David I as a comparatively modest structure, rebuilt between 1195 and 1230 on a much grander scale. The new building was erected around the old Abbey, allowing it to continue in use until the new Abbey was completed, after which the old building was demolished. It was extensively damaged during the Hertford Invasion of 1544 but renovated again in time for Charles I's coronation of 1633. After a serious roof fall in 1768, the Abbey entered a long period of neglect, resulting in its present-day appearance as a romantic ruin. Restoration schemes proposed in 1906 and again in 1945 came to nothing.

Holyrood as a royal residence probably dates from the latter part of the fifteenth century. Between 1501 and 1505 James IV built a new palace (probably incorporating some of the monastic buildings) and the work was continued by his son, James V, between 1528 and 1532. The building which we see today, however, is largely the work of Charles II's Master Mason, Robert Mylne, who began reconstruction in 1672. Holyrood was greatly re-enforced as a royal residence in 1822 during George IV's visit to Scotland, even though he opted for the overnight comforts of Dalkeith Palace. At the present day, the Queen and several members of the Royal Family make frequent use of the Palace, particularly during the Queen's annual official visit in June or July, and also for the General Assembly of the Church of Scotland, held annually in May.

In the lower half of the picture a lot of development has taken place since the photograph was taken in 1994. Immediately opposite the Palace forecourt, the buildings of Scottish & Newcastle Breweries have been demolished for the construction of the Scottish Parliament. Between Holyrood Road and the Royal Park, two large feus of ground have been changed out of all recognition. The square site is now Our Dynamic Earth and the one with the two circular gasometer bases is now the headquarters of Scotsman Publications Ltd. Much of the north side of Holyrood Road has also been cleared and redeveloped as housing, hotels and offices.

Left. One of the engineers responsible for the reconstruction of No. 4 Meadow Flat Gas Holder on the south side of Holyrood Road in 1933.
Crown copyright: RCAHMS ref. B/37263.

Right. A young visitor studying the information trolley at the entrance to Our Dynamic Earth in Holyrood Road in 1999.
Crown copyright: RCAHMS ref. D/68257.

1. Holyrood Abbey
2. Holyrood Palace
3. Scottish & Newcastle Breweries
4. Site of Our Dynamic Earth
5. Site of Scotsman Headquarters
6. Holyrood Road

Inner Suburbs

Abbeyhill

Belford

Bruntsfield

Dalkeith Road

Dalry

Fountainbridge

Gorgie

Grange

Greenhill

Lauriston

Marchmont

Meadows

Merchiston

Newington

Polwarth

Salisbury

Sciennes

Stockbridge

West Coates

Crown copyright: RCAHMS ref. E4093.

Easter Road and the Abbeyhill colonies, 2002, looking towards Holyrood Palace, the Scottish Parliament under construction, Our Dynamic Earth and Salisbury Crags.

CHAPTER 2

Cox's Glue Works, 1930

The centre of the photograph is dominated by Cox's Glue Works which appear as blocks of light coloured geometric shapes on the south side of Gorgie Road. These are the open-air pans, or ponds, in which the animal hides and skins were soaked for several weeks to remove the worst of the impurities and make them more supple for the first stage of glue-making. The raw materials came from several abattoirs throughout Scotland. Cox's Glue Works was established at Linlithgow in 1725 but moved within a relatively short time to Bell's Mills at the Dean village. The firm settled at Gorgie in 1798 where it remained until 1969. For almost two and a half centuries Cox's presence was keenly felt by everyone who lived near its strong-smelling processes. Unfortunately, in 1969 Cox's ceased production of its high-grade glue, gelatine and other related products, a victim of changed markets and different economic considerations. The site of the glue works is now occupied by Telephone House on the south side of Gorgic Road.

Several railway tracks are visible at the top of the picture. The track, running from left to right across the picture, serves the slaughterhouses at Gorgie, and the one curving off the top of the picture is part of the suburban line near Gorgie Station. To the left of Cox's Glue Works is the U-shaped building of St Nicholas Special School and to the left again is the gymnasium of Gorgie Public School. The main school building, dating from 1871 (later used as Tynecastle Annexe) is nearer to Gorgie Road. The original 'tin school', Gorgie Special School (replaced in an annexe to the south of St Nicholas) also shows in the picture between the gymnasium and Gorgie Road. Below the line of Gorgie Road are numerous business premises, including Didcock Bros, furniture makers, first established at Cramond around 1896. Adjacent to Didcock's is the seventeenth-century Gorgie House which was demolished in 1937.

Left. No self-respecting cook was ever without Cox's Manual of Gelatine Cookery. A leaflet of 'delightful recipes' was enclosed in every packet of gelatine.
Courtesy of Mrs Jean Moffat.

Right. Ada McArthur at the door with her brother, Jackie and his dog, Billy, in the front garden of their home, Gorgie House, *c.* 1932. For many years the McArthur family ran a Riding Academy from the stables adjacent to the house.
Courtesy of Mrs Sheila Scott.

1. Suburban line
2. Gorgie Public School
3. Gymnasium
4. St Nicholas Special School
5. Tin School
6. Cox's
7. Gorgie Road
8. Gorgie House

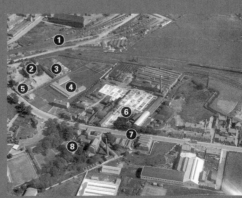

1. Union Canal
2. Dalry House
3. Dundee Street
4. Dalry Station
5. Dalry Church
6. Dalry School
7. Dalry Motive
   Power Depot
8. Coffin Lane
9. Dalry Road
10. Dalry Cemetery

Dalry Station, 1930

Dalry railway junction is the dark-coloured triangular area in the centre of the picture. The roof and platform of Dalry Station is on the left of the triangle, and Dalry Sheds, (officially known as Motive Power Depots) for the maintenance of the engines, is on the right. The main Caledonian Railway line out of Princes Street Station runs through the junction and under Dundee Street at the awkward road alignment on the extreme right of the picture. To the left of Dalry Station there is a siding to serve the premises of Alexander Mather, engineers, in Orwell Terrace, and Colin Macandrew, Public Works Contractors in West End Place. The line of the old Caledonian Railway is now the West Approach Road to Lothian Road.

Dalry Road runs diagonally across the bottom left-hand corner of the photograph. Dalry Primary School and Dalry Parish Church (now demolished and replaced by a modern church building, St Colm's) are on the corners with Cathcart Place. On the right of Dalry Road, and nearer to Haymarket, is

the seventeenth-century Dalry House in Orwell Place. Dundee Street runs diagonally in the top right-hand corner, much of the ground covered, in the photograph, by McEwan's Brewery now laid out as the leisure centre, Fountain Park. The Union Canal and the North British Rubber Co. Ltd, established in 1855, is in the top right-hand corner.

Above. Railway workers at Dalry Sheds, one of the maintenance depots of the Caledonian Railway.
Courtesy of Bill Forrest.

Left. Colin Macandrew & Partners Ltd, Public Works Contractors, had their office and yard at West End Place from 1919 to 1967. Among their many Edinburgh contracts were Redford Barracks and the National Library of Scotland on George IV Bridge.
Courtesy of the author.

Stockbridge, 1930

St Stephen's Parish Church, in the centre of the picture, was designed by William H. Playfair, and its clock was fitted with the longest pendulum in Europe. The church was opened in 1828 and closed in 1992 when the congregation united with St Bernard's Stockbridge in Saxe Coburg Street (previously West Claremont Street) to form Stockbridge Parish Church. St Stephen's clock tower, rising 162 feet, completely dwarfs the much more modest St Vincent's Episcopal Church, seen to the right at the head of St Stephen Street. On the curved section of the street, nearest to St Stephen's Church, is the Grand Picture House, used in the 1980s as Cinderellas Rockerfellas, and later demolished following a serious fire. Also visible in St Stephen Street are the three, light-coloured pitched roofs of St Stephen's Mission Hall, now converted into flats.

Hamilton Place is near the bottom of the picture, running left to the junction with West Claremont Street (now Saxe Coburg Street), Henderson Terrace and Claremont Street. In Hamilton Place, Stockbridge Primary School was opened in 1877, and Stockbridge Library in 1898. There are two other educational establishments in the bottom left-hand corner of the picture. The square building, designed by James Gillespie Graham, was opened in 1824 as the Institution for the Education of Deaf and Dumb Children. It was in existence before Donaldson's Hospital at Wester Coates, which did not open until 1850, but in 1939, almost a decade after this picture was taken, the two schools amalgamated to form Donaldson's School for the Deaf. In July 1968, the Henderson Row building was temporarily converted to the 'Marcia Blaine School for Girls' for the filming of *The Prime of Miss Jean Brodie.* The other, larger building, the Edinburgh Academy, sits back from the line of Henderson Row. The Academy was the brainchild of Henry Cockburn (later Lord Cockburn) and Leonard Horner with enthusiastic backing from John Russel WS and Sir Walter Scott. The low, single-storey building, with the central, pillared portico, was designed by William Burn to a budget of £13,000. The school was opened on 1 October 1824 with 372 boys enrolled. Silvermills lies between the Academy and St Stephen's Church: its name dates from the sixteenth century when ore from a small silver mine at Linlithgow was brought to the village for refining. In recent years the area has been extensively redeveloped.

Members of the Navy and Army Canteen Board, and a few onlookers, on the steps of St Stephen's Parish Church on 2 August 1919, before going on their annual picnic to Blackness Castle.

Courtesy of the author.

1. St Stephen's Church
2. St Vincent's Church
3. Silvermills
4. Grand Picture House
5. St Stephen's Mission
6. Edinburgh Northern Tram Depot
7. Public Wash-house
8. Edinburgh Academy
9. Institute for Deaf Children
10. Stockbridge School
11. St Cuthbert's Co-op
12. Stockbridge Library

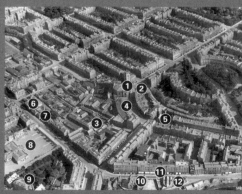

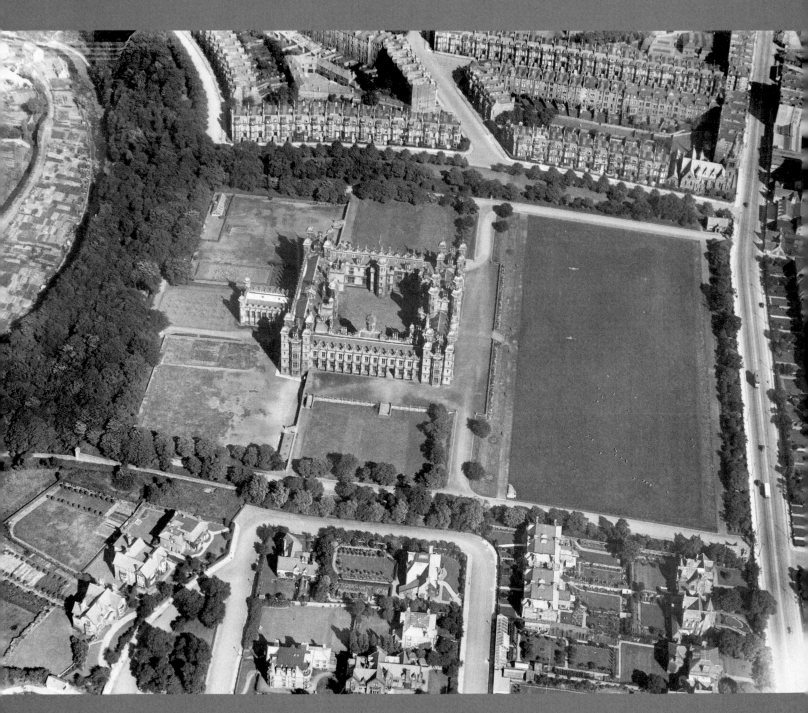

1. West Coates Church
2. Magdala Crescent
3. Donaldson's Hospital
4. West Coates
5. Wester Coates Gardens

Donaldson's Hospital, 1930

The magnificent quadrangle of Donaldson's Hospital at West Coates was designed by the architect, William H. Playfair who also designed several other notable buildings in Edinburgh, including the art galleries on the Mound and the National Monument (intended to be a copy of the Parthenon) on Calton Hill. Donaldson's Hospital, as it was first named, was built of stone from Craigleith and Binny quarries by Young & Trench between 1842 and 1851. The photograph shows the hospital from the west with the chapel (now used as the school hall) projecting from the rear of the building. It is set in open grounds, remarkably uncluttered by ancillary buildings, bounded, on the north by the Water of Leith, on the south by West Coates, on the east by Magdala Crescent, and on the west by Wester Coates Gardens.

Donaldson's Hospital was founded after the death, in 1830, of James Donaldson, publisher and printer of West Bow, who left the sum of £210,000 'to build and found an hospital for boys and girls to be called Donaldson's Hospital preferring those of the name Donaldson and Marshall to be after the plan of the Orphan Hospital in Edinburgh and John Watson's Hospital'. Pupils were first admitted on 16 October 1850. For almost a century Donaldson's Hospital maintained a separate identity to its sister organisation in Henderson Row, the Institution for the Education of Deaf and Dumb Children. However, in 1939 the two schools combined to form Donaldson's School for the Deaf, senior pupils being taught at West Coates and junior pupils at Henderson Terrace. From 1977 seniors and juniors were both taught at West Coates.

The church on the east corner of Magdala Crescent and Haymarket Terrace is West Coates, opened in 1870. When it united with Roseburn Church in 1962 to form Wester Coates, the Roseburn building was used for worship and the West Coates building was demolished and replaced by an office block, not in harmony with the surrounding buildings.

Drawing of Donaldson's Hospital by William H. Playfair and D. Roberts from the north-west.

Crown copyright: RCAHMS ref. EDD/232/45.

Union Canal, 1930

The Union Canal runs diagonally from the top left-hand corner of the picture, at the Lochrin Basin, then curves to its left as it passes Harden Place at the bottom of the picture. Towards the end of the eighteenth century, several speculative reports were compiled on the possibility of linking Edinburgh and Glasgow by a ship canal suitable for freight and passenger services. In 1813 Hugh Baird compiled a *Report on the Proposed Edinburgh and Glasgow Union Canal* in which he explained the line of the canal, the technical difficulties, and the estimated costs and expected revenues. The total cost of the canal, basins, aqueducts and reservoirs was estimated at £235,167 but by the time the canal was opened in 1823 the cost had risen to £461,760.

To the left of the canal is the North British Rubber Company Ltd, established in 1856 by Henry Lee Norris who brought four employees to Edinburgh from the USA to start the business. They sailed to Scotland in the windjammer *Harmonia* to begin the manufacture of boots and shoes in what had been Castle Silk Mills on the north bank of the canal. It was not long before the business was well established, eventually extending its range of products to include motor car tyres, conveyor belts, combs, golf balls, hot water bottles and rubber flooring.

Also to the left of the canal are the streets of Temple Park, and North Merchiston School, dating from 1882, in Bryson Road. Gilmore Place, Granville Terrace and Polwarth Gardens lie almost parallel to the canal. Between Harden Place and Polwarth Place, allotments occupy the ground on which Polwarth Park was built in the early 1930s. Rather surprisingly, there is a gap in the tenements on the east side of Harden Place. In the photograph the ground is occupied as a builder's yard, owned by William Graham, who lived at Maharg in Oxgangs Road. The steeple of the John Ker Memorial Church can be seen in Polwarth Gardens. The church was built in 1893, to designs by David Robertson, in memory of Rev. Professor John Ker, DD, but was demolished after the union with Candlish Church in 1981.

To the right of Polwarth Gardens are the villas of West Castle Road, East Castle Road and Merchiston Avenue. Beyond Merchiston Avenue are: St Oswald's Church, built in 1900 in Montpelier Park; Bruntsfield Primary School, built in 1893 in Montpelier; and Boroughmuir School, built in 1911 in Viewforth.

The Union Canal, photographed in 1939 from below the Viewforth bridge, looking east to the Leamington lift bridge at Gilmore Park, with numerous boathouses on the south bank.

Crown copyright: RCAHMS ref. ED/3357.

1. North British Rubber Co.
2. Boroughmuir School
3. St Oswald's Church and
   Bruntsfield School
4. John Ker Memorial Church
5. Harden Place
6. North Merchiston School
7. Union Canal
8. Allotments

1. Donaldson's Hospital
2. Dalry Road
3. Murrayfield
4. Edinburgh–Glasgow railway
5. Tynecastle Park
6. Shandon Bridge
7. Gorgie Road
8. Suburban railway

Gorgie and Dalry, 1941

At first glance, this general view of Gorgie and Dalry, looking north-east, is a confusing conglomeration of streets and railway lines, some of which have long since been closed. The long, straight, dark-coloured line of the Edinburgh to Glasgow railway runs from the left-hand edge of the photograph to the top right-hand corner at Haymarket. Above the line of the railway are: Murrayfield, the centre of Scottish Rugby Union, on the left; and Donaldson's Hospital, on the right. One of the arterial roads into the City begins at the bottom edge of the picture (Gorgie Road) and runs approximately parallel to the Edinburgh to Glasgow railway, past Tynecastle, home of the Heart of Midlothian Football Club, until it reaches Ardmillan where it becomes Dalry Road. Slateford Road is in the bottom right-hand corner, crossing the suburban railway line west of Robertson Avenue, and then over the Caledonian link to Haymarket, at Shandon Bridge.

On Monday, 20 October 1941 when this photograph was taken by the Royal Air Force, the industrial character of the area is evident from the many chimney stacks. From left to right, some of the larger firms are: Cox's Glue Works in Gorgie Road; Macfarlan Smith, Chemicals, in Wheatfield Road; North British Distillery also in Wheatfield Road; Robert McVitie, Biscuits, in Robertson Avenue; T. & J. Bernard's Edinburgh Brewery in Slateford Road; and the Caledonian Brewery, also in Slateford Road. During the war years many firms in Gorgie and Dalry were working on Government contracts in support of the war effort, and others had their production seriously altered. In December 1939, normal production at the North British Distillery was halted owing to lack of raw materials and manpower, most of the employees having been called up to the armed services. For the duration of the war years (until 1945) the company had no option but to concentrate on developing its by-products department, particularly with the introduction of North British Golden Grains, a nutritious form of cattle feed. Normal production was gradually re-introduced after 1945.

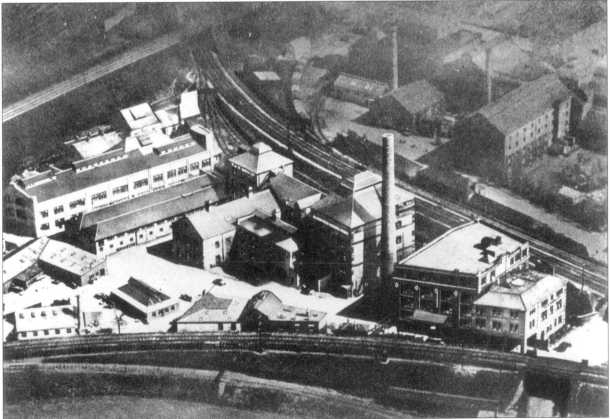

Macfarlan Smith Ltd., manufacturer of fine chemicals and natural extracts, occupies the extensive Blandfield works situated within the triangle of land between the railway lines at the north end of Wheatfield Road. From *A History of T. & H. Smith Ltd,* 1952.

Thirlestane and Whitehouse, 1951

The long, straight line of Thirlestane Road, with only one parked vehicle, meets Whitehouse Loan in the bottom left-hand corner of the picture. The building of Thirlestane Road (between Whitehouse Loan and Spottiswoode Street) was commenced in 1878 at the west end by Robert Chisholm and John Davidson but the partnership appears to have been dissolved by the time Robert Chisholm completed the work in 1900. In Whitehouse Loan, the detached house, facing down Thirlestane Road, was called Oakvale until the 1930s when St Margaret's Convent renamed it St Crescentia's as part of their boarding school. To the left of Oakvale is Warrender Church, designed by R. Macfarlane Cameron, and opened in 1892. After the church closed in 1972 at the union of Warrender, West St Giles' and Grange to form Marchmont St Giles' Church, the Warrender building was converted to residential accommodation.

Half-way down Thirlestane Road, on the right, is the long pitched roof and tall chimney for Warrender Baths. The Baths were opened on Saturday 17 December 1887 by Sir George Warrender of Lochend who had feued the piece of ground on which the baths were built to the Warrender Private Baths Co. Ltd. The cost of the building and the equipment was £11,000.

St Margaret's Convent, which pre-dates the building of Marchmont and Greenhill, occupies the large piece of open ground in the centre of the picture. The convent was founded in 1834 by the Sisters of the Ursulines of Jesus in the seventeenth-century property known as the Whitehouse which was incorporated into the convent. The photograph shows the Whitehouse abutting Whitehouse Loan, behind which is St Margaret's Chapel, designed by the architect, James Gillespie Graham, in 1835, and the detached houses, the Hermitage (on the left) and St Margaret's Tower facing Strathearn Road.

This building was erected in 1891 as Warrender Park Free Church and renamed United Free in 1900. The congregation became part of Marchmont St Giles' Church in 1972.
Courtesy of the author.

Warrender Park U.F. Church, Edinburgh.

1. Warrender Baths
2. St Margaret's Tower
3. The Hermitage
4. St Margaret's Chapel
5. The Whitehouse
6. Whitehouse Loan
7. Oakvale
8. Warrender Church

1. Barclay Church
2. Gillespie's School
3. Gillespie's Hospital
4. Darroch School
5. Boroughmuir School
6. Viewforth Church
7. St Kentigern's Church

Gilmore Place to Marchmont, 1951

The lower half of the picture shows the area of the Union Canal looking south-east to Bruntsfield Links. This mixed area of commercial and residential properties is typical of the development of Edinburgh during the nineteenth century. The upper part of the photograph, in much less detail, includes the districts of Marchmont, Sciennes and the Grange.

The North British Rubber Co. Ltd was established on the north bank of the Union Canal in 1855 and produced a vast quantity of boots, shoes, tyres and golf balls among many other items, for well over a century. Four school buildings (giving them their 1951 name) are also evident: James Gillespie's High School for Girls in Warrender Park Crescent; Boroughmuir Senior Secondary School in Viewforth; Darroch Intermediate School in Gillespie Street; and the first Gillespie's Hospital (School) in Gillespie Crescent which was occupied by the Royal Blind Asylum School when this photograph was taken. There are also several churches of various denominations, also given their 1951 name. The most dominant spire is Barclay in Barclay Place, to the right of which is Bruntsfield in Leamington Terrace. Nearer to the bottom of the picture is Viewforth with its tower complete; the Free Presbyterian Church in Gilmore Place (near Darroch School); and the Convent of the Little Sisters of the Poor in Gilmore Place. The very small St Kentigern's Church, originally a mission station from St John's Episcopal Church at the West End, is also shown on the south bank of the Union Canal.

Left. The interior of St Kentigern's Church in St Peter's Place, originally a mission station for St John's Episcopal Church at the West End. The church, designed by the architect, Dick Peddie, was reached from a pend on the east side of St Peter's Place. *Courtesy of George and Edith Fraser.*

Bottom. The staff of Boroughmuir Senior Secondary School in 1954 at the time of the fifty-year anniversary. In the front row (9th from the left) is the headmaster, R.L.S. Carswell, flanked by his heads of department, one of whom (6th from the left) is the Gaelic poet, Sorley Maclean, who was head of English. From *Boroughmuir Jubilee 1904–1954*, published in 1954.

Sciennes and the Grange, 1951

Sciennes Road, which marks the north boundary of the former Grange estate, runs almost vertically on the left of the picture, beginning at Argyle Place Church. Hatton Place is to the right of the church, with Chalmers Crescent, Mansionhouse Road, Lauder Road and Tantallon Place running between it and Grange Road. The congregations of Argyle Place Church and St Catherine's in Grange (on the corner of Chalmers Crescent and Grange Road) began very differently but were united in 1968 to form St Catherine's Argyle Church. St Catherine's in Grange began as a Free Church around 1861 but the Grange Road building was not opened until 1866. The Argyle Place Church congregation (United Presbyterian) was formed in 1877 and the foundation stone was laid on 1 November 1879 by the Lord Provost of Glasgow, William Collins. Prior to the union of the two congregations in 1968, a decision had been taken to use the Argyle Place building for worship and the Grange Road building as hall accommodation. Unfortunately, this plan had to be altered when Argyle Place Church was seriously damaged by fire in 1974 as a result of which it was demolished.

To the left of Sciennes Road, several non-residential buildings are located in an area which is otherwise occupied mainly by tenement buildings. The first is the Royal Hospital for Sick Children, opened on 31 October 1895 on the site of the former Rillbank House which had been the home of the Trades Maiden Hospital. Prior to 1895, the Sick Children's Hospital had been at Meadowside House on the north side of the Meadows. In the photograph, to the left of the main building, is the stack for the hospital laundry which was in Sylvan Place. Sylvan House, dating from before 1750, can also be seen in the shadow of the Sylvan Place tenements. Sciennes Primary School, designed by the Edinburgh School Board architect, Robert Wilson, was built on the site of Millerfield House, and opened on 1 March 1892. Beyond the school building, the pitched roofs at the corner of Sciennes Road and Sciennes are Bertram's, engineers and manufacturers of paper-making machinery.

Right. Argyle Place Church on the corner of Sciennes Road and Chalmers Crescent in 1952. In 1974 the building was seriously damaged by fire as a result of which it was demolished.
Courtesy of the late Mrs Betty Gwilt's family.

Below. The staff of Bertram's, engineers, on the roof of their St Katherine's Works in Sciennes, c. 1950.
Courtesy of the author.

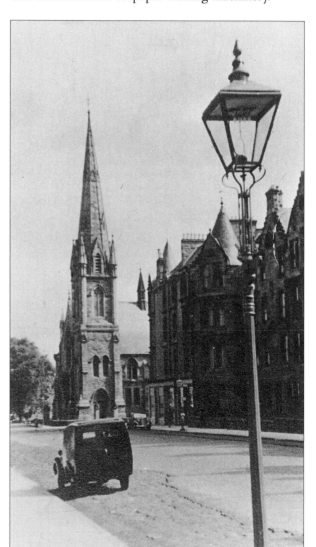

1. Bertram's
2. Grange Road
3. St Catherine's Church
4. Sciennes School
5. Sick Children's Hospital
6. Sciennes Road
7. Hatton Place
8. Sylvan House
9. Argyle Place Church

1. C & J Brown's warehouse, now RCAHMS
2. St Peter's Episcopal Church
3. Newington Road
4. Nurses Home
5. Longmore Hospital, now Historic Scotland
6. Minto Street

Minto Street and Newington Road, 1951

The north end of Minto Street is in the foreground of the picture, leading onto Newington Road at the junction with Salisbury Place, to the left, and Salisbury Road, to the right. When the photograph was taken in 1951 traffic at the junction was being controlled by a policeman on points duty from the nearby Braid Place Police Station. Braid Place was subsequently renamed Sciennes House Place and the old police station was converted into flats. Minto Street was first laid out around 1807 with many of the grand houses built in the period to 1830, but greatly altered by later generations.

The long white building in Salisbury Place is the Longmore Hospital, financed by a gift of £10,000 from John Alexander Longmore WS of Deanshaugh, and opened on 10 December 1880 by Sir Thomas Jamieson Boyd, Lord Provost of Edinburgh. The hospital was built on the site of the much smaller Edinburgh Hospital for Incurables at No. 8 Salisbury Place and was extended in 1886 and again in 1898. After closure of the Longmore Hospital in the early 1990s the building became the headquarters of Historic Scotland which has responsibility for Scotland's built heritage. The square, five-storey, white building in Salisbury Road was designed in 1935 by the architect, J. Douglas Miller as the Longmore Hospital Nurses Home but has recently been converted to residential use.

Further into the picture is St Peter's Episcopal Church in Lutton Place dating from c. 1860. Behind it (in the photograph) is Bernard Terrace on the south side of which is a warehouse belonging to C. & J. Brown, House Furnishers. The building was renovated in the early 1990s as the new home of the Royal Commission on the Ancient and Historical Monuments of Scotland, opened on 11 May 1992 by the Chairman of the Commission, The Rt Hon. the Earl of Crawford and Balcarres.

Below left. Changing shifts on points duty at the junction of Salisbury Road and Minto Street in the early 1930s. On the left is PC Alexander Norrie and on the right is PC John Kennell.
Courtesy of the late Mrs Helen Davidson (née Norrie)

Below right. When this photograph was taken c. 1910, Salisbury Road was a private street with bollards across the junction with Dalkeith Road. The shop on the corner was A. Ross, Egg and Butter Merchant at No. 44 Dalkeith Road.
Courtesy of the author.

Meadows, Sciennes and the Grange, 1961

Vertical aerial photographs of the city provide a very clear view of the open spaces, arterial roads and feuing plans which all contribute to the character of a district. The Meadows, with part of the ground given over to allotments, are located in the top left-hand corner of the picture, to the right of which are two main roads out of the city: the one on the extreme right is Clerk Street and the other is Buccleuch Street and Causewayside. The tree-lined curve running across the picture below the line of the Meadows is Melville Drive. Grange Road, running west from Causewayside, was initially intended as an access road only to Grange Cemetery, laid out in 1847 by the Edinburgh Southern Cemetery Company.

At one time, the area covered by the East and West Meadows was occupied by the Burgh, or South, Loch. During the sixteenth century it was one of the principal sources of water for the inhabitants of the Old Town, but it was also used by the people living beside it to wash clothes and water their horses. It was not until 1676 that clean drinking water was piped into the city from Comiston Springs. After several unsuccessful schemes, the loch was eventually drained and the land laid out as an ornamental park by Thomas Hope of Rankeillor from 1722.

The district of Sciennes, to the south of Melville Drive, is a mixture of tenement buildings and non-residential development, which includes Sciennes Primary School and the Royal Hospital for Sick Children. The large, dark-coloured industrial unit to the left of Causewayside is Bertram's, manufacturers of paper-making machinery. After the firm closed, the buildings were demolished in 1987 and the ground redeveloped as flats. The district of Grange lies to the south of Sciennes. It takes its name from the sixteenth-century Grange House which lay to the south of Dick Place. Although the original house had been greatly enhanced by the Dick-Lauder family in the nineteenth century it fell into a poor state of repair and was demolished around 1936. The villas of the Grange, seen in the bottom half of the picture, were laid out under the direction of the Dick-Lauders in a series of feuing plans from 1825.

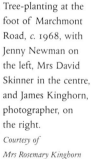

Tree-planting at the foot of Marchmont Road, *c.* 1968, with Jenny Newman on the left, Mrs David Skinner in the centre, and James Kinghorn, photographer, on the right.
Courtesy of Mrs Rosemary Kinghorn

1. Allotments
2. Meadows
3. Clerk Street
4. Melville Drive
5. Bertram's
6. Causewayside
7. Grange Cemetery
8. Grange Road

1. Eye Pavilion
2. Biology Building
3. Florence Nightingale Nurses Home
4. Central clocktower and Surgical block
5. Simpson Maternity Pavilion
6. Jubilee Pavilion
7. Medical Pavilions

Royal Infirmary of Edinburgh, Lauriston, 1989

Plans were considered around 1870 to move the Royal Infirmary of Edinburgh from its site in Infirmary Street to Lauriston Place. One of the many problems was that the Lauriston Place location was by no means a greenfield site. It was already occupied by several important buildings, all in their own grounds, which were eventually swept away as the Infirmary tightened its grip on the site. The buildings included George Watson's School (partly retained), Wharton House, the Sick Children's Hospital, and the Merchant Maiden Hospital. The first part of the Infirmary at Lauriston was designed in the Scottish baronial style by the architect, David Bryce, from 1872, and after his death in 1876, by his nephew, John Bryce. The central clock tower faces Lauriston Place, flanked on each side, and to the rear, by six surgical blocks. The medical pavilions, on the south side overlooking the Meadows, were opened in 1897, and the adjacent Diamond Jubilee Pavilion in 1900. The most significant twentieth-century buildings (other than the piecemeal additions to almost everything) are all on the west side of the complex: the Florence Nightingale Nurses Home, 1935; the Simpson Memorial Maternity Pavilion, 1935; the Eye Pavilion, on the west side of Chalmers Street, 1971; and the square, white Reproductive Biology Building, with the central ventilation flues, 1977.

Below top. Lauriston House, built in the early 1960s, was demolished in 2002. *Photograph by Phyllis M. Cant.*

Below. This 1966 photograph of Lauriston illustrates how much the area has changed over the years. From left to right: the light-coloured, wedge-shaped 1960s building, Goldberg's Store, has been demolished; the glass and concrete box, built for the National Coal Board at the top of Lady Lawson Street, has been demolished; above it, the motor garages of John Croall & Sons Ltd, at the foot of Johnston Terrace have been demolished and replaced by Argyle House; and on Lauriston Place, to the right of the Fire Station, the ugly shop fronts have been swept away and the site greatly enhanced, in the early 1970s, by the Hunter Building of the Edinburgh College of Art. *Crown copyright: MoD ref. 58/RAF/7537, 0033.*

Dalkeith Road, 1989

The centre of the picture is dominated by the hexagonal composition designed in 1972 by Basil Spence, Glover & Ferguson as the headquarters of the Scottish Widows Fund and Life Assurance Company (now Scottish Widows PLC). The company was founded in Edinburgh in 1815 and employs over 4,500 people worldwide, the majority of whom are based in Scotland. The very distinctive brown glass building was constructed on the site of the printing works of Thomas Nelson & Sons. Thomas Nelson, born near Bannockburn in 1780 started as a bookseller in Edinburgh in 1798 and soon extended his business into printing religious tracts and larger books in monthly parts. His first factory was at Hope Park but following a serious fire in 1876 the entire firm was moved to the Parkside Works in Dalkeith Road. Holyrood Park Road separates the Scottish Widows building from the Royal Commonwealth Pool which was designed, with an Olympic-standard pool, by Robert Matthew, Johnson-Marshall & Partners in time for the 1970 Commonwealth Games.

Dalkeith Road runs diagonally from the top of the left-hand edge of the photograph to the bottom right-hand corner. Preston Street Primary School is on the corner of Dalkeith Road and East Preston Street. Beyond, and on the opposite side of the road, is the former St Leonard's Church dating from 1880.

It united with Newington Church in 1932 and the combined congregation was dissolved in 1976. Newington Burying Ground, immediately opposite the Scottish Widows building, was laid out *c.* 1820 when St Cuthbert's Kirk Session purchased the ground from Mr Handyside for the sum of £1,800. The new cemetery was intended to replace the cemetery around Buccleuch Parish Church which the authorities had declared as overcrowded. The small building in the corner of the cemetery ground was the Newington Session School, later used as a staff canteen by Nelson's.

Right. The Dalkeith Road site in 1961 showing Nelson's printing works on the north side of Holyrood Park Road, and playing fields on the south side where the Royal Commonwealth Pool now stands.
Crown copyright: MoD ref. 58/RAF/4488 F21, 0160.

Below. The Parkside Works of Thomas Nelson & Sons was demolished *c.* 1970 to make way for the headquarters of the Scottish Widows Fund.
Courtesy of the author.

1. Former St Leonard's Church
2. Holyrood Park Road
3. Preston Street School
4. Scottish Widows
5. Newington Burying Ground
6. Former Newington Session School
7. Dalkeith Road
8. Commonwealth Pool

1. Haymarket Railway Station
2. Caledonian Distillery
3. Dalry Road
4. Dalry House
5. West Approach Road
6. Scottish & Newcastle Breweries

Dalry and Caledonian Distillery, 1993

At one time almost all the ground in this photograph formed part of the Lands of Dalry which stretched from the Edinburgh to Glasgow railway line (near the top of the picture) to Dundee Street in the bottom right-hand corner. Rather remarkably, the manor house, Dalry House, built in 1661, remains in what is now Orwell Place. Originally there were two access driveways from Dalry Lane (now Dalry Road) and one from Fountainbridge which crossed the line of the Caledonian Railway (now the West Approach Road).

The Haymarket road junction is in the top right-hand corner, with Haymarket Station slightly to the left of the junction. When the Glasgow to Edinburgh railway line was built in 1842 it terminated at Haymarket and was not extended to Waverley until 1846. The large industrial site with the tall chimney, between the railway line and Dalry Road is the Caledonian Distillery established in 1855 on what was then a greenfield site. There were other factors which influenced the decision to locate at Dalry. The site lay between the lines of the Caledonian Railway and the Edinburgh & Glasgow Railway, both of which provided branch lines which led into the works. In addition, the Union Canal was relatively close, providing a gravity-fed supply of water for cooling which was carried in an underground pipe nearly a mile long. The distillery closed in 1987, a few years before this photograph was taken. The small white building between the Caledonian Distillery and the station buildings is Easter Dalry House which is believed to be slightly older than Dalry House.

Below the line of Dalry Road are the tenement buildings of Orwell, and the distinctive arc of Caledonian Crescent, the rear windows of the houses looking out over the West Approach Road, previously the Caledonian Railway line. The industrial area in the bottom right-hand corner of the picture is Scottish & Newcastle Breweries, part of which has now been redeveloped as the leisure and cinema complex, Fountain Park.

A hostelry has stood on the site of the present Ryrie's Bar at Haymarket for many years. It was the Haymarket Inn from at least as early as 1862 and the premise were remodelled for Messrs Ryrie & Co. in 1906.
Courtesy of the author.

Slateford Road and North Merchiston Cemetery, 1993

The large group of trees in the centre of the picture is North Merchiston Cemetery, the foliage masking most of the headstones which date from 1874. Running almost vertically on the left of the picture is the main railway line to Carlisle which branches off the Glasgow line west of Haymarket Station. Slateford Road, leading onto Angle Park Terrace, crosses from bottom left to top right, and Gorgie Road cuts off the top left-hand corner of the picture.

Two important developments lie between Gorgie Road and North Merchiston Cemetery. On the left is Gorgie Farm, established in 1982 on land previously used by Edinburgh Corporation Cleansing Department. The refuse lorries tipped their contents into railway waggons on a small siding communicating with the main track. The second development is the complex on the corner of Gorgie Road and Ardmillan Terrace first laid out in 1864 as the Edinburgh Magdalene Asylum, later renamed Springwell House.

St Michael's Parish Church, designed by the Glasgow architect, John Honeyman, and opened in 1883, sits on the gusset of land between Slateford Road and Harrison Road. The long straight line of trees to the right of St Michael's marks the position of the former Caledonian Railway line which is now a walkway and cycle path. Two industrial units are near the bottom of the picture. On the left, the Caledonian Brewery, founded by George Lorimer and Robert Clark in the late 1860s, is wedged between the railway and Slateford Road, and, on the right, the square of pitched roofs was Weston's Biscuit Factory. Below the line of Weston's are the Slateford colonies built in 1877.

The piggery at Gorgie City Farm is ever popular, especially with the youngest generation. The farm, opened in 1982, attracts over 100,000 visitors each year.
Courtesy of Gorgie Farm.

1. Gorgie Farm
2. Railway
3. St Michael's Parish Church
4. Slateford Road
5. North Merchiston Cemetery
6. Weston's (previously)
7. Caledonian Brewery
8. Slateford colonies
9. Former Caledonian Railway

PART TWO

COLOUR SECTION

George IV Bridge, looking north, across the junction with the Lawnmarket, to the headquarters of the Bank of Scotland. Beyond, Festival visitors are crowded around the art galleries and on the terraces of East Princes Street Gardens. Photographed in 1994. *Crown copyright: RCAHMS ref. C40333 CN.*

The ancient spine of the Old Town of Edinburgh, crossed by the North and South Bridges in the foreground, and continuing uphill past St Giles' Cathedral and the law courts to Edinburgh Castle at the head of Castlehill. Photographed in 1985. *Crown copyright: RCAHMS ref. A40710 CN.*

Greyfriars Kirk, surrounded by its ancient graveyard, is in the centre of the picture. The graveyard dates from 1562 but the building of the church was not started until 1611. It was opened in 1620. Heriot's School, in the top right-hand corner, was started in 1628 and completed around 1650. Photographed in 1994. *Crown copyright: RCAHMS ref. C40354 CN.*

The individual buildings in Craig's New Town of Edinburgh, between Princes Street and Queen Street, have been radically altered over many years but none has destroyed the overall sense of proportion to the same degree as St James Centre and New St Andrew's House. Photographed in 1985.

Crown copyright: RCAHMS ref. A40709 CN.

Looking in a north-easterly direction over Edinburgh Castle, the Gardens and Princes Street. Work has just started on the Standard Life building on Lothian Road. In Princes Street, the Palace Hotel, on the corner of Castle Street, has been demolished following a serious fire, and the steel-work for the new office building is being erected. Photographed in 1994. *Crown copyright: RCAHMS ref. C40330 CN.*

Moray Place, in the centre of the photograph, is generally considered to be one of the most elegant spaces in the north-west section of the New Town. It was built, along with the smaller oval-shaped Ainslie Place and Randolph Crescent between 1822 and 1836. Charlotte Square is on the right of the picture. Photographed in 1994. *Crown copyright: RCAHMS ref. C40309 CN.*

St Mary's Episcopal Cathedral, at the west end of Melville Street, dominates this view of the western
New Town, first laid out in the early nineteenth century. The two double crescents are Eglinton Crescent
and Glencairn Crescent, on the left, and Grosvenor Crescent and Lansdowne Crescent on the right.
Coates Crescent and Atholl Crescent are in the top right-hand corner. Photographed in 1994.

The distinctive Caledonian Hotel (now Caledonian Hilton Hotel), built of warm red sandstone, has a long frontage to Lothian Road and a shorter frontage to Rutland Street. In recent years Edinburgh's financial centre has moved progressively south from its traditional home in and around George Street. The Standard Life building takes pride of place on the corner of Lothian Road and the West Approach Road. The Usher Hall is on the left of Lothian Road and the Sheraton Grand Hotel lies to the right of Festival Square. Photographed in 1999. *Crown copyright: RCAHMS ref. D56518.*

The area between the West Approach Road and Tollcross continues to attract major new building development. The semi-circular building in the foreground is Scottish Widows PLC; the complete circle is the Edinburgh International Conference Centre; and the long T-shaped buildings in the top left-hand corner are Exchange Tower (on the left) and Caledonian Exchange (on the right). Photographed in 1999. *Crown copyright: RCAHMS ref. D56515.*

The square enclosure on the left of Calton Hill contains the City Observatory and Observatory House, with the Dugald Stewart monument outside the perimeter wall. The pillars of the National Monument give scant protection to the Fringe production, the Jim Rose Circus Sideshow, to the right of which is the Nelson Column. Photographed in 1994. *Crown copyright: RCAHMS ref. C40332 CN.*

The undulations in the fairways of Prestonfield Golf Course were never intended as additional hazards: they are, in fact, signs of ground cultivation, medieval in origin. Beyond the golf course are Prestonfield House Hotel and the circle stables. The line of the Innocent Railway can be seen between the golf course and the low road around the Royal Park. Photographed in 1999.

Crown copyright: RCAHMS ref. D32945 CN.

Holyrood as a royal residence probably dates from the latter part of the fifteenth century. The ruined Abbey to the left is very much more ancient, having been founded in 1128 by David I, and rebuilt between 1195 and 1230. Scottish & Newcastle Breweries, with the cars in the quadrangle, has since been demolished for the construction of the Scottish Parliament. Photographed in 1994.

Crown copyright: RCAHMS ref. C40350 CN.

Less than a decade later than the previous photograph, both sides of Holyrood Road have been transformed by new buildings, by far the most dominant being the new Scottish Parliament, taking shape on the site previously occupied by Scottish & Newcastle Breweries. Photographed in December 2002. *Crown copyright: RCAHMS ref. D50409.*

The Old Quad of Edinburgh University on South Bridge is in the centre of the picture, adjacent to the Royal Museum of Scotland. The new Museum of Scotland has yet to be built. McEwan Hall and the Royal Infirmary are in the top left-hand corner. Photographed in 1985.

The photograph shows South Bridge where it crosses over the Cowgate. The blackened area in the centre is the site of the serious fire which caused widespread damage to the fabric of several buildings on the evening of Saturday, 7 December 2002. Photographed shortly after the fire was extinguished.
Crown copyright: RCAHMS ref. E12552 CN.

The Stockbridge colonies were constructed from 1861 by the Edinburgh Co-operative Building Co. Ltd. The various streets are named after the principal participants in the original company: Hugh Miller, Hugh Gilzean Reid and James Colville. The large modern building at the top of the picture is Standard Life's Tanfield headquarters. Photographed in 1994. *Crown copyright: RCAHMS ref. C40363 CN.*

The Royal Botanic Garden Edinburgh moved to Inverleith in 1823 although its origins go back to 1670 when a small Physic Garden was begun near Holyrood Abbey. The temperate Palm House, opened in 1858, is in the centre of the picture and remains, to this day, the tallest in Britain. Adjacent is a long range of modern glasshouses. The rectangular, white building is the Herbarium, opened in 1964. Photographed in 1994. *Crown copyright: RCAHMS ref. C40360 CN.*

Cramond, looking north-east towards the Firth of Forth, with the River Almond on the left. Cramond Kirk dates from 1656 with a fifteenth-century tower from a previous church. Also in the picture, nearer to the shore, are the sixteenth-century Cramond Tower and the larger seventeenth-century Cramond House to the right. The outline of the Roman fort lies in the triangle of ground between the Kirk and Cramond Tower. Photographed in 1985. *Crown copyright: RCAHMS ref. A40687 CN.*

In 1511, the *Great Michael*, flagship of the Scottish Navy, was launched at Newhaven at a time when the port was to be developed as the Royal Dockyards. At the present day most of the subsequent fishing fleet has long since gone but it is still a popular mooring place for pleasure craft. Photographed in 1994.
Crown copyright: RCAHMS ref. C40292 CN.

The photograph shows, to the south of Liberton Drive, the last-surviving Second World War anti-aircraft battery in the Edinburgh area. The large circle (originally octagonal) is the remains of a GL (gun laying) mat which incorporated a radar unit. Below the line of the unit, the four small circles are gun emplacements, formed around the command centre. The two adjacent rectangular buildings are the magazines. Photographed in 2002. See also page 120 for comparison. *Crown copyright: RCAHMS ref. E/12558/CN*

PART THREE

North

Crown copyright: RCAHMS ref: E04086 CN.

The Royal Yacht *Britannia* was commissioned by King George VI and was launched, after his death, from John Brown's Shipyard at Clydebank in 1953. After travelling more than one million miles to many parts of the globe, she was decommissioned on 11 December 1997 and was brought to Leith in 1998, where she has attracted over a million visitors. Since this photograph was taken, in 2001, the Royal Yacht has been moved to her present-day position along the quayside at Ocean Terminal.

Leith Docks, 1930

The photograph, dated 29 July 1938, shows the East Breakwater under construction, part of more extensive works to create a wider and deeper entrance to the port. The construction of the breakwater, under the direction of J. D. Easton, M.Inst.C.E., President of the Institute of Civil Engineers and Superintendent Engineer of Leith Docks, was modelled on the Great Dyke which enclosed the Zuyder Zee. The Dutch engineers employed at Leith were all arrested (probably unnecessarily) at the outbreak of the Second World War and the project was not restarted until May 1941.

Courtesy of David Easton.

The Port of Leith has a long and eventful history, first mentioned in the twelfth-century charters of David I. As early as the middle of the sixteenth century it was evident that the entrance to the port was in need of improvement, but it was not until the eighteenth century that the first stone pier and graving dock were built. During the nineteenth century, however, Leith was transformed into a well-equipped port, able to deal with vast quantities of imports and exports. East Old Dock was built between 1800 and 1806, followed by West Old Dock between 1810 and 1817. By 1851 the east and west piers had been greatly extended to create a sheltered outer harbour. The second part of the nineteenth century saw considerable expansion to the east, including, Victoria Dock (1851), Albert Dock (1863), Edinburgh Dock (1881) and Imperial Dock (1893).

By the time this photograph was taken in 1930 there were fourteen shipping companies advertising out of Leith, including the famous Currie Line and Salvesen. The main shipbuilders included Ramage & Ferguson Ltd, Henry Robb Ltd, John Menzies & Co. Ltd, and George Brown & Sons. Shipping routes were established to all the main United Kingdom ports as well as Europe, America, Africa, Canada, India, China, Japan and Australia. Coal, at nearly two million tons annually, was the leading bulk export. Imports included corn, wine, wool, fruit and vegetables.

The photograph shows predominantly the older parts of the port. West Old Dock is on the right with both its dry docks unoccupied. Above West Old Dock is a small part only of East Old Dock, to the left of which is the full expanse of Victoria Dock. Victoria Dock communicates directly with the Outer Harbour on the seaward side of the Victoria Swing Bridge which can be seen in the top right-hand corner of the picture. In the centre of the picture, the long, light-coloured sheds are part of Henry Robb's shipyard which has several vessels under construction. At the top of the picture, above the line of the Outer Harbour, are the entrances to two other docks. The long narrow lock, on the left, opens out into Imperial Dock in which there is one fairly large vessel. To the right of the adjacent sheds is a smaller vessel, with a light-coloured bridge, moored at the Albert Dock Basin. The basin gives access to a lock for Albert Dock and Edinburgh Dock which are off the top edge of the picture.

1. Imperial Dock
2. Albert Dock Basin
3. Victoria Swing Bridge
4. Outer Harbour
5. Victoria Dock
6. Ramage & Ferguson
7. East Old Dock
8. Henry Robb's Yard
9. West Old Dock

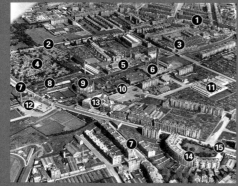

1. Leith Walk
2. Pilrig Street
3. Shrubhill Tram Depot
4. Rosebank Cemetry
5. LNER to Granton
6. Power station
7. Broughton Road
8. Brown Bros
9. Gasometer
10. McDonald Road
11. T. & A. Constable
12. Refuse disposal plant
13. Broughton Schools
14. Claremont Crescent
15. East Claremont Street

Broughton Road and East Claremont Street, 1930

A great variety of commercial and industrial buildings, many of them serviced by the railway network, is contained within the area bounded by East Claremont Street, Broughton Road, Pilrig Street and Leith Walk. East Claremont Street runs from the bottom right-hand corner of the picture, past the curved terraced buildings of Claremont Crescent, to meet Broughton Road which continues past Rosebank Cemetery to the junction with Pilrig Street. Pilrig Street runs from the cemetery to Pilrig Church at the junction with Leith Walk near the top right-hand corner of the picture.

Running parallel to Pilrig Street, but much nearer to the gasometer, is the London & North Eastern Railway (LNER) to Granton Harbour and Leith Docks. To the right of the gasometer, in McDonald Road, are the premises of William Taylor & Co., Soap Powder Manufacturers, and further right again, the Electricity power station (with the high chimney) opened in 1899. To the right of the power station, the chimney stack beside two rows of pitched roofs, is Shrubhill Tram Depot entered from Leith Walk. The engineering works of Brown Brothers & Co. Ltd, Rosebank Ironworks, lie between Rosebank Cemetery and the railway. The high, smoking chimney on the left-hand side of the picture belongs to Edinburgh Corporation's refuse disposal plant.

The façade to Broughton Road has a central tower and symmetrical flanks of red sandstone, designed by the City Architect, John Cooper, in 1893.

Diagonally opposite, on the corner of McDonald Road, are the two Broughton Schools. The older building, facing into Broughton Road, is the primary school opened as Broughton Public School in 1896. It was designed by Robert Wilson, the School Board architect, and is still in use at the present day. The other building, with the long frontage into McDonald Road, was designed by Wilson's successor, John A. Carfrae, in 1902. From 1904 it was known as Broughton Higher Grade School and subsequently became Broughton Secondary School which moved to Carrington Road, opposite Fettes College, in 1972.

On the extreme right of the picture, the light-coloured pitched roofs are the almost new works of T. & A. Constable Ltd, Printers, in Hopetoun Street, who can trace their origins back to 1760. The Hopetoun Street premises were opened in 1929 after the firm had outgrown its Thistle Street buildings. In a short history of the firm published in 1936, the description of the modern works concludes with the comment: 'Although the majority of the employees reside at no great distance from the works, a Mess-room controlled by a Works Committee is provided.'

This 1943 photograph of the same area shows the gasometer with its wartime camouflage paint, making it considerably less conspicuous from the air, but by no means invisible. Air raid shelters can be seen to the rear of Broughton School and also in the bottom left-hand corner of the picture.

Crown copyright: RCAHMS (RAF Collections) ref. D50276.

Leith Walk and Leith Central Station, 1951

This early twentieth-century photograph of 'the Foot o' the Walk' shows: Smith & Bowman, Chemists, on the extreme left; Queen's Hotel and Restaurant on the corner of Constitution Street; and Leith Central Station with North British Railway notice boards on the outside wall. The open-topped tram was run by Leith Corporation Tramways who had electrified their line up to Pilrig Street before their Edinburgh counterparts. The elegant lampposts and overhead line supports were also specifically designed for Leith.
Crown copyright: RCAHMS ref. ED7235.

The road junction, near the bottom of the picture, is the north end of Leith Walk leading to Great Junction Street, Kirkgate, Constitution Street and Duke Street. The pitched glass roofs of Leith Central Station are on the right, dwarfing the small station clock tower which was a landmark at 'the Foot o' the Walk' for many years. Leith Central Station, which had wooden platforms, was Edinburgh's third largest station. It was opened in 1903 and closed in 1952, a year after this photograph was taken. It occupied the whole length of Duke Street from Leith Walk to Easter Road. When the station was opened by the North British Railway one of the first services was every half-hour to Waverley Station.

Leith Links are on the right of the picture, criss-crossed by various paths. The Links are of great antiquity, firstly as an area of common grazing and then as one of Scotland's ancient homes of golf dating from at least the early seventeenth century. Leith Academy has had a significant presence adjacent to the Links for many years. In 1888 the former Leith High School in St Andrew Place was renamed Leith Academy, and in 1896 the old High School building was demolished and replaced by a new building on the same site, designed by George Craig. This is the substantial building with the central tower on the right of the

picture. When the St Andrew Place building became too small, a new secondary school was built at the south-east end of Duke Street, and the primary department remained at St Andrew Place.

The photograph also shows the spires of several churches in the district, by far the most ancient being South Leith which lies between Kirkgate and Constitution Street. Its origins go back to 1483 but much of the present-day structure is the result of Thomas Hamilton's remodelling of 1848. Three other churches can be seen in Constitution Street. Slightly north of South Leith Church (and on the same side of the road) is St Mary Star of the Sea Roman Catholic Church, designed in 1852 by E. W. Pugin and Joseph A. Hansom, but substantially altered over the years. On the opposite side of the street, and sitting back from the pavement, is St James Episcopal Church, 1862, now in secular use. The tower parapet of St John's East Church, also in secular use now, can be seen further north than St James.

Finally, to the left of Leith Academy in St Andrew Place, is the rear view of St Andrew Place Church opened in 1827 at a cost of £5,000. In 1973 the congregation united with Leith Claremont in Easter Road to form Leith St Andrew's and used the Easter Road building for worship.

1. St John's East Church
2. St Mary RC Church
3. St James Episcopalian Church
4. Bonded warehouse
5. Leith Links
6. South Leith Church
7. Constitution Street
8. St Andrew Place Church
9. Leith Academy
10. Kirkgate
11. Great Junction Street
12. Central Station
13. Duke Street
14. Leith Walk

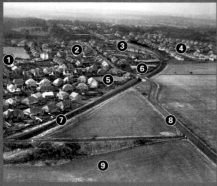

1. Davidson's Mains School
2. Davidson's Mains village
3. Davidson's Mains goods yard
4. Silverknowes
5. Bowling club
6. Springfield Nursery
7. LMS railway
8. Ferry Road
9. Drylaw estate

Davidson's Mains, Silverknowes and Drylaw, 1951

The photograph shows Davidson's Mains on the left, Silverknowes on the right and the Drylaw estate, still undeveloped, nearest to the camera. The three districts are separated by the Barnton branch of the London, Midland & Scottish Railway (LMS) which shows in the picture as a dark-coloured line starting in the bottom left-hand corner, running under Ferry Road, and then swinging to the left as it passes the village of Davidson's Mains. There was a station and a small goods yard at Davidson's Mains, and a station at Barnton where the line stopped. Passenger services ceased in 1951. The distinctive bend where Ferry Road negotiates the railway line is still evident today but the track has long since been lifted and the route made into a public walkway and cyclepath. To the left of Ferry Road, as it enters the village, is the clubhouse and green of the Maitland Bowling Club formed in 1899, and taking its name from the Maitland family who owned the ground on which it was built. To the right of Ferry Road are the extensive glasshouses of the Springfield Nursery run by James Bruce & Son.

Davidson's Mains Primary School, in Corbiehill Road, is on the extreme left of the picture beside the open field. The school was opened as a Board School in 1874 and was expanded in 1907 by the addition of an extra building which communicated with the original school. Both buildings were demolished and replaced by a new primary school on the same site, opened on 25 April 1967 by the Right Rev. R. Leonard Small, Moderator of the General Assembly of the Church of Scotland.

Part of the Drylaw estate is in the foreground of the picture. The estate dates from at least the early fifteenth century when it was owned by the Forrester family of Corstorphine. Later owners of the estate included James Loch, who built Drylaw House in 1718, and William Ramsay of Barnton.

This photograph of Drylaw House was taken from the same sortie, a few frames before the main photograph opposite. The most obvious point of reference between the two is the awkward bend in Ferry Road as it crosses the railway. Drylaw House, which still stands in Groathill Road North, was built by James Loch in 1718. When this photograph was taken on 7 December 1951 it was still surrounded by its estate, with a walled garden and greenhouse on the south side.
Crown copyright: MoD ref. 58/RAF/813,0225, SFFO.

1. Chancelot Mill
2. Ferry Road
3. Clark Road
4. St Serf's Church
5. Heriot's playing field
6. South Trinity Road
7. Fulton's Garage
8. Trinity Cottage
9. Rose Park
10. Larkfield
11. LMS railway to Leith North
12. Wardie Road

Bangholm, Ferry Road, 1951

Wardie Road runs from left to right across the bottom of the picture. Running parallel to it is South Trinity Road (near the centre of the picture) and then Clark Road which meets Ferry Road at St Serf's Church on the right of the picture. The railway, starting in the bottom right-hand corner and curving towards the top left-hand corner, connected Granton Road Station, Newhaven and Leith.

The area between Wardie Road and South Trinity Road has several houses of historical interest, described in detail by Joyce M. Wallace in *Further Traditions of Trinity and Leith*, first published in 1990. To the right of the railway, two adjacent properties are quite different in architectural style. The taller building with the crow-stepped roofs is Trinity Cottage, built in 1894 by the Leith shipowning family, Currie, of Currie Line, as their private house. After the Second World War, the house was used as an office for Currie Line and was later demolished for the construction of the government building, Trinity Park House, in 1969. Adjacent to Trinity Cottage, the slightly older, lighter-coloured building with the turreted corner is Larkfield. It too was demolished to build Trinity Park House. Larkfield was entered from Wardie Road where the lodge house survived the 1969 demolition but was later taken down for residential development.

To the left of the railway, the low-pitched white roofs are the premises of R. Fulton & Co., Motor Engineers, of South Trinity Road. The garage was built on the site of a large detached house, Newbank, which later included two smaller properties nearer to South Trinity Road. One was North Newbank and the other was Newbank South. At the present day North Newbank has been demolished but Newbank South survives, apparently incorporating parts of a much older building. Another mansion, Rose Park, can be seen in the picture, partly hidden by trees, between Fulton's Garage and Wardie Road. This extensive, eighteenth-century house was demolished in 1962 but the coach house and stables, which probably served Newbank as well as Rose Park, survived, and were later renovated as private houses.

In the background, the distinctive building with the tall stack and clock tower is Chancelot Mill, built by the Scottish Co-operative Wholesale Society Ltd, and used for many years for the production of 'Lofty Peak' flour. The mill was relocated to Leith Docks in 1954 and Chancelot Mill was demolished in 1972.

Top. Chancelot Mill, built by the Scottish Co-operative Wholesale Society Ltd, produced 'Lofty Peak' flour for many years until the business was moved to a new mill at Leith Docks in 1954. The building seen here was not demolished until 1972. From *Leith and its Antiquities*.

Left. The unusually shaped, light-coloured building in the centre of the picture is Trinity Park House, built on the site of Trinity Cottage in 1969. Photographed in 1991.

Crown copyright: RCAHMS ref. B/69905.

Inverleith and Canonmills, 1991

Inverleith Row runs almost vertically from the bottom edge of the picture to Canonmills near the top of the picture. To the left of Inverleith Row is Warriston Drive, Eildon Terrace, Eildon Street and Warriston playing fields.

The extensive wooded and cultivated ground to the right is the Royal Botanic Garden Edinburgh laid out at Inverleith in 1823. The Botanic Garden can trace its roots to 1670 when Dr Andrew Balfour and Dr Robert Sibbald established a Physic Garden on a small piece of ground, St Anne's Yard, near Holyrood Abbey, with James Sutherland as the first head gardener. In 1675, by which time the garden had outgrown the available space, the collection of plants was moved to a larger piece of ground beside Trinity Hospital, near where Waverley Station was later built. The Garden remained there until 1763 when it was moved to a five-acre site off Leith Walk, now occupied by Haddington Place. The final move was to Inverleith in 1823. In the photograph the rectangular building with the light-coloured roof is the Herbarium, opened in 1964, which can be seen in colour, along with the other main buildings of the Garden, on page 87. The history of the development of the Garden and the involvement of many eminent botanists is told in *The Royal Botanic Garden Edinburgh, 1670–1970* by Harold R. Fletcher and William H. Brown.

The modern building, towards the top of the picture, is the Tanfield headquarters of the Standard Life Assurance Company, occupying a seven-acre site straddling the Water of Leith. The building was designed by the Michael Laird Partnership and opened on 1 July 1991 by Her Majesty Queen Elizabeth II. The main building consists of four floors: the basement is used as a car park; the ground and first floors are open-plan offices lit by three atria; and the second floor has the dining area which communicates with the rooftop garden. The smaller building on the south side of the Water of Leith is the Data Centre. Standard Life was founded as the Life Insurance Company of Scotland on 23 March 1825 at No. 200 High Street, Edinburgh. It changed its name to the Standard Life Assurance Company in 1832, and moved, in 1839, to No. 3 George Street which, at the present day, is used by the company's investment department.

Tanfield had an interesting history before the days of Standard Life. During most of the nineteenth century it was home to the Oil Gas Company and the Edinburgh Gas Company, both of which had rather unsightly gasometers on the site. Tanfield Hall, which had formed part of the Oil Gas Company's buildings, was the historic location of the Disruption in 1843 when almost one-third of the ministers, elders and members of the Established Church of Scotland, dissatisfied with the system of patronage in the appointment of ministers, broke away to form the Free Church of Scotland.

Inverleith Terrace runs at right angles to Inverleith Row, nearer to the camera than Tanfield. The substantial building, standing in its own grounds, is the Church of Scotland's St Colm's College, designed by Gordon L. Wright in 1908.

The printing works of Morrison & Gibb Ltd, in Howard Place, were demolished for the construction of Standard Life's Tanfield headquarters opened in 1991. On the right of the picture, the façade of the old wool warehouse was saved and incorporated into the new building.
Photograph by the late A. L. Hunter.

1. Canonmills
2. Standard Life
3. Standard Life
4. St Colm's College
5. Inverleith Terrace
6. Warriston Ground
7. Eildon Street
8. Inverleith Row
9. Botanic Garden
10. Eildon Terrace
11. Warriston Drive
12. Herbarium

South

Alnwickhill

Blackford

Colinton

Craiglockhart

Dreghorn

Fairmilehead

Firrhill

Glenlockhart

Grange

Greenbank

Juniper Green

Liberton

Meggetland

Morningside

West Mains

West Savile

Crown copyright: RCAHMS ref. D50416 CN.

Looking in a south-easterly direction, from above the houses in Comiston Drive, towards the ski slope on the Pentland Hills. The Braid Hills are on the left of the picture and Braidburn Valley Park is in the centre. Photographed in 2002.

Craiglockhart Hydropathic, Convent of the Sacred Heart, 1930

The sweeping curve of Colinton Road divides the picture horizontally. In the upper half, the most dominant building, in the style of a giant Italian villa by the architects Peddie & Kinnear, was built on the west side of Wester Craiglockhart Hill between 1877 and 1880 as Craiglockhart Hydropathic. In the early 1870s the Craiglockhart Estate Company feued thirteen acres of ground to the newly formed Craiglockhart Hydropathic Company which was obliged by the terms of the feu charter to erect a building within three years to a value not less than £10,000. In the late nineteenth century hydropathics were becoming very popular, and Craiglockhart, with its proximity to the city, was ideally placed to become a popular resort. Outdoor activities extended to tennis, archery, croquet and bowls whilst indoor activities included billiards, reading and card rooms, and a large heated swimming pool. During the First World War, when the Hydropathic was requisitioned as a military hospital, its patients included the War poets Wilfred Owen and Siegfried Sassoon. In 1920 the building became the Convent of the Sacred Heart and in 1984 it was bought by the then Napier College. The College was awarded University status with degree-awarding powers in 1994.

To the left of the Hydropathic are the steadings of Craiglockhart Farm, demolished in 2002, and the remains of Craiglockhart Castle in Glenlockhart Road. Farther along Glenlockhart Road, on the left, is the west lodge to the City Poorhouse. Several tennis courts are also visible at Happy Valley in the top left-hand corner of the photograph. Below the line of Colinton Road some of the bungalows of Craig-lockhart are still in the course of erection with feus on the main road not yet taken.

1. Tennis courts
2. West Lodge
3. Craiglockhart Farm Steading and Castle
4. Hydropathic
5. Colinton Road
6. Hillcrest

1. Greenbank Farm steading
2. Greenbank Drive
3. City Poorhouse
4. City Hospital
5. Merchants Golf Course

City Hospital and City Poorhouse, 1930

The road in the centre of the picture, running diagonally from top left to bottom right, is the upper section of Greenbank Drive. All the buildings to the left of the road are the Edinburgh City Poorhouse and those to the right are the City Hospital.

The Poorhouse was designed in the Scottish baronial style by George Beattie in 1865 to replace very cramped accommodation previously in use at Forrest Road. In the new building at Glenlockhart males and females were strictly separated, except in the dining room and the chapel. Even in the dining room the men were kept to the west side, separated from the women on the other side by 'a low screen, not too high so as to injure the appearance of the hall or give it a prisonlike appearance'. The building plan was basically a series of pavilions arranged around a central clock tower with the male dormitories on the west side and the female dormitories on the east. The

Poorhouse later became Greenlea Old People's Home until the 1980s when the buildings were redeveloped as private housing known as The Steils.

The City Hospital was designed by the City Architect, Robert Morham, and opened on 13 May 1903 by Lord Provost, James Steel. By 2000 the City Hospital was also at an early stage of redevelopment for private housing. The history of the City Hospital is told by Dr James A. Gray in a very scholarly but readable style in *The Edinburgh City Hospital* published in 1999.

The upper part of the photograph shows the first of the houses in Greenbank Crescent and the house and steadings of Greenbank Farm. Shortly after this photograph was taken the fields were being marked out for the streets of Greenbank. Part of the Merchants of Edinburgh Golf Course can be seen on the left of the picture.

Mrs Margaret Scott and her daughter, Violet, at Greenbank Farmhouse *c.* 1923. Mrs Scott was housekeeper to Dick Boa the last tenant farmer at Greenbank.
Courtesy of Mrs Violet Gordon, née Scott.

West Mains Road and King's Buildings, 1930

West Mains Road, with trees on both sides, runs almost vertically in the picture to meet Mayfield Road coming diagonally, from left to right. King's Buildings are in the process of construction on the large site to the right of West Mains Road. The largest building, with the two rows of pitched roofs, is the Chemistry Block (now the Joseph Black Building) completed between 1920 and 1924. Next to that (going towards Mayfield Road) is the Geology Block (now the Grant Institute) completed shortly after this photograph was taken showing it under construction. The angle-shaped Zoology Block (now the Ashworth Laboratories) was constructed on the corner of West Mains Road and Mayfield Road from 1927 to 1928. The last building, in Mayfield Road, is the Engineering Block (now the Sanderson Building) built between 1929 and 1932. Almost opposite the Engineering Block is Hallhead Road running north-east towards Gordon Terrace. Several building plots have been marked out on both sides of Hallhead Road but very few have been developed.

Towards the bottom of the picture there are other buildings below the access road off West Mains Road. The right-hand group has a two-storey T-shaped building constructed in 1929 to house the Animal Genetics Department (now the Crew Building) adjacent to the piggeries, the sheep house and the goat house. The other group of buildings, Liberton West Mains, was in existence long before King's Buildings: the farmhouse can be seen surrounded by trees on the left-hand side of West Mains Road and the farm steadings are on the right-hand side. The site of the old farmhouse is now occupied by a garage on the corner of West Mains Road and Langton Road. The open ground at the bottom of the picture, to the right of West Mains Road, was used for the construction of the British Geological Survey in 1971. In 1930 the Survey was at South Park in Grange Terrace.

West Mains Road looking west towards the Harrison Arch and the Royal Observatory. The Harrison Arch was designed in 1887 in appreciation of the work done by Lord Provost George Harrison in acquiring the Blackford Hill for the benefit of the public.
Courtesy of the author.

West Mains Road & Observatory, Edinburgh.

1. Engineering Block
2. Zoology Block
3. Geology Block
4. Chemistry Block
5. Animal Genetics Block
6. Liberton West Mains Farm
7. Liberton West Mains Farmhouse
8. Later site of British Geological Survey

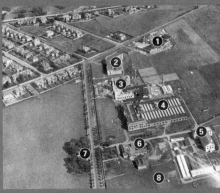

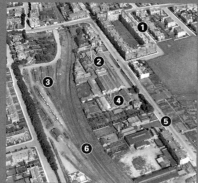

1. Macdowall Road
2. Craigmillar Steam Laundry
3. Goods Yard
4. Ward
5. West Savile Terrace
6. Suburban line

West Savile Terrace, 1930

The railway track in the centre of the picture is the suburban line (closed to passengers in 1962 but still used for freight) between Blackford Station and Newington Station. The small goods yard with access from Mayfield Road is now occupied by Relugas Gardens. The long straight road to the left of the railway line is Relugas Road and the one to the right of the track is West Savile Terrace, both of which meet Mayfield Road at the top of the picture. In 1930 most of the area between the railway and West Savile Terrace was occupied by commercial and industrial premises. The largest building, with the factory chimney and pitched roofs (nearest to Mayfield Road) is Craigmillar Steam Laundry Ltd. West Savile Motors, a subsiduary of the laundry company, was begun in part of the premises in 1958 with a filling station constructed on the forecourt. The next building, also with a tall chimney, was Ward, Printers, later W. R. Annan, also printers, and then Macgregor & Co. (Glass & China) Ltd. Others in the section include the Scottish Moulding Company, Hope's Laundry and the North British Rubber Company.

To the right of West Savile Terrace allotments occupy the site of present-day Langton Road. In the top right-hand corner of the picture is Macdowall Road only partly completed with four-storey tenements on the north side and terraced villas on the south side. To the right of Macdowall Road, and running parallel to it, is Ross Gardens, also partly completed.

Macdowall Road looking east towards its junction with Mayfield Road. *Courtesy of the author.*

Macdowall Road.

M. 3

Dreghorn Barracks, 1940

This vertical view of Dreghorn Barracks shows the site almost equally divided by an access road (running vertically in the photograph) from Redford Road. To the left of the access road is the original Victorian barrack block which still remains as the centrepiece of the modern barracks. The parade ground is to the north of the Victorian block. To the right of the access road is an extensive hutted camp, parts of which remained until the mid-1980s when the complex was redeveloped. This camp, with camouflaged roofs on the huts, was used as transit accommodation during the Second World War. When the photograph was taken the barracks was empty: the troops based there at the time were probably deployed to France as part of the British Expeditionary Force, and evacuated from Dunkirk between 26 May and 4 June 1940, a few weeks before this photograph was taken. The top right-hand corner of the photograph shows that practice trenches had already been dug near to the trees.

The hamlet of Fordel can be seen just off Redford Road on the right of the picture. At one time Fordel had three houses: Fordel Cottage used by the gamekeeper to the Dreghorn estate; a cottage with a pantiled roof used as a military post office by the army during the First World War; and a smaller thatched cottage used by an estate gardener. Fordel Cottage was the most substantial building, of significant historical importance, which was unfortunately demolished around 1985. On its side wall there was a lengthy inscription cut into a stone tablet commemorating General Gordon.

Right. The Covenanters' Monument close to the entrance to Dreghorn Barracks in Redford Road, was constructed from the columns from the old Royal Infirmary in Infirmary Street after it was demolished c. 1884.
Photograph by Phyllis M. Cant.

Below. When this photograph was taken, probably in the 1930s, Fordel belonged to the War Department. The sign reads: 'THIS IS W. D. PROPERTY AND IS CLOSED TO THE PUBLIC'.
Courtesy of the author.

1. Practice trenches
2. Redford Road
3. Access road
4. Fordel
5. Victorian block
6. Hutted camp

1. Craigmillar Park Golf Course
2. Liberton Tower
3. Liberton Drive
4. Mount Vernon Cemetery
5. Village
6. Liberton House
7. Gun battery
8. Filter beds

Liberton and Alnwickhill Filter Beds, 1946

The lower part of the photograph shows Alnwickhill Reservoir and filter beds which were built by J. & A. Leslie, Engineers, between 1875 and 1885. Water reaches the main reservoir of twenty million gallons (on the left) from the Tala, Crawley and Moorfoot pipes and falls, by gravity, to the twelve slow sand filter beds, before entering the freshwater storage tanks for consumers on the east side of Edinburgh.

On the right of the picture is the old village of Liberton clustered around Liberton Kirk, built in 1815 on the site of a much earlier church. Liberton Kirkyard can be seen clearly on the left side of the village and Mount Vernon Cemetery on the right side. When the photograph was taken, in 1946, there were still many fields and open spaces between the various arterial roads.

The unusual circular shape to the left of the filter beds, and to the south of Liberton Drive forms part of a heavy anti-aircraft gun battery position from the Second World War, the only one in Edinburgh to survive to the present day. The circular area was originally octagonal, and was known as a GL (gun laying) mat, incorporating a radar unit, centrally positioned, to enable the gunners to determine the height and range of an incoming aircraft. The gun-emplacements can be seen (below right of the circular area) as four small semi-circles with the command centre in the middle. The accommodation camp of Nissen, and wooden, huts is on the left. A colour photograph of the site in 2002 appears on page 90.

To the right of the gun battery position, surrounded by trees, is the sixteenth-century Liberton House (recently restored by the architects Nicholas Groves-Raines), and to the north of Liberton Drive, the even older Liberton Tower (recently restored by the architects Simpson & Brown) and now used as a holiday house. The high-walled fortress of Liberton Tower was built by the Dalmahoy family who later sold it and the surrounding ground to the Littles. The original plan for the Tower was a four-storey rectangular block with a pitched roof of stone slabs surrounded by a parapet walk. When the Little family thought they were no longer in need of a defensive position they moved out of Liberton Tower and built the much more elegant Liberton House on the south side of what is now Liberton Drive.

Looking north across the Alnwickhill filter beds towards the square, pinnacled tower of Liberton Kirk in the centre of the old village.
Courtesy of the author.

Liberton from Edinburgh Water Works.   M. 421.

Blackford Hill, 1946

Blackford Hill fills the bottom left-hand quarter of the picture, criss-crossed by numerous informal paths. The group of buildings on the right of the hill is the Royal Observatory, built in 1894 with two green copper cylinder towers, a library block, and later additions in 1967. Evidence of much longer-term human occupation on Blackford Hill is known from the remains of a small fort on Corbies Crag. In addition to that, most of the area to the left of the Observatory is covered with rig-and-furrow cultivation, just visible as light and dark lines between the later informal paths. To the right of the Observatory is Craigmillar Park Golf Course, the natural contours of the ground spoiled by the encroachment of Blackford Quarry which is no longer producing stone. The large complex to the right of Blackford Hill is King's Buildings in West Mains Road (see page 115).

The upper half of the picture is the district of the Grange, laid out in successive feuing plans from the mid-nineteenth century. Immediately to the right of Carlton Cricket Club ground is the vacant site of Grange House (dating from at least the seventeenth century) which was demolished a decade before this picture was taken. Nothing remains of the house in the picture but the layout of the garden ground is just discernible before it was redeveloped as Grange Crescent.

1. Carlton Cricket Club
2. Site of Grange House
3. Royal Observatory
4. King's Buildings
5. Craigmillar Park Golf Club
6. Blackford Quarry

1. Merchiston Castle School
2. Heather Cottage
3. Colinton Kirk
4. Mackenzie's Cottage
5. Village
6. Redford Barracks

Colinton Village, 1951

Almost the entire village is shown in the bottom centre-left part of the picture, with the south-facing tower and gables of Colinton Kirk reflecting the low sunlight. The present church building, surrounded by an ancient graveyard, dates from 1908, but stands on the site of previous ecclesiastical buildings believed to date from 1095. In 1908 a major reconstruction of the church was done by the architect, Sydney Mitchell, who rearranged the gables and reused the square tower over the new entrance porch. The manse, seen to the right of the church, was frequently visited by Robert Louis Stevenson whose maternal grandfather, Rev. Dr Lewis Balfour, was minister of the parish from 1823 to 1860.

Bridge Road leads uphill through the village, past Henry Mackenzie's cottage (author of *The Man of Feeling*) to Heather Cottage on Colinton Road. Heather Cottage was built around 1810 as part of Colinton House estate. Its gables, raised above the line of the slates, and the dripstones at the base of the chimneys, confirm that this quaint old cottage was once thatched. Firrhill and Craiglockhart Hill are in the extreme top right-hand corner of the picture. The extensive, wooded policies, occupying most of the centre of the picture, are the grounds of Merchiston Castle School which is set well back from the roadway. Merchiston Castle School was previously at Merchiston Tower, now part of Napier University at Holy Corner in Morningside, but transferred to the Colinton site in 1930.

When this picture was taken in 1951 Colinton was served by the electric tramway system to a terminus at the junction of Bridge Road and Woodhall Road. Two tram cars can just be seen to the left of Heather Cottage. Redford Barracks lies to the south of Colinton Road before it reaches Firrhill. The Cavalry Barracks (nearest to Firrhill) and the Infantry Barracks (nearest to Colinton) were built between 1909 and 1915 by Colin Macandrew & Partners, the Edinburgh public works contractors, who constructed a light railway to bring stone and timber to the site from Slateford Station.

Entrance to Colinton village in 1870 with Colinton School behind the trees on the left. The Rev. Dr Lewis Balfour (grandfather of Robert Louis Stevenson) was minister at Colinton from 1823 until his death in 1860. The photograph shows Colinton as R.L.S. would have known it before he left Edinburgh in 1887.
Courtesy of the late Miss E.D. Robertson's family.

Mrs Helen Dickson outside her house, Heather Cottage, in 1940, collecting her groceries from the Juniper Green Co-operative delivery man, who was her son, William Dickson.
Courtesy of Mrs Maggie McConnell.

Morningside, 1989

This unusual view of Morningside was taken from above Hermitage Gardens, looking in a north-westerly direction, with the suburban railway line curving from the bottom right-hand corner to the top left-hand corner. The main road junction at Morningside Station is in the centre of the picture with Comiston Road running to the left and Morningside Road running to the right.

Ecclesiastical Morningside is represented by three substantial church buildings which, at one time, had three separate congregations. On the extreme right is Braid Church, designed by George Washington Browne, and opened in 1887 as Braid United Presbyterian Church. In 1990, the year after this photograph was taken, Braid Church and Morningside Parish Church (not in the photograph) united to form Morningside Braid Parish Church. In the bottom left-hand corner of the picture two churches were opened within a few years of one another towards the end of the nineteenth century. St Matthew's, designed by Hippolyte Blanc, was opened in 1890 and South Morningside Free Church was opened in 1892: they united in 1974 to form Cluny Parish Church. Shortly, Morningside Braid and Cluny will also unite, bringing the four previous congregations under one roof.

Morningside Cemetery, laid out in 1878, is in the top left-hand corner of the picture between Balcarres Street and Morningside Drive. It is the burial place of several eminent citizens: William Cowan, a past President of the Old Edinburgh Club who bequeathed a valuable collection of books and papers on Edinburgh to the Central Public Library; Alison Cunningham, 'Cummy', Robert Louis Stevenson's nurse; and in much more recent years, Sir Edward Appleton, Principal of Edinburgh University. In 1981 members of the Morningside Association compiled a detailed *Survey of Monumental Inscriptions in Morningside Cemetery*.

Morningside Road Station on Wednesday, 14 May 1958, looking east on the suburban railway which was closed to passenger services in 1962. The two traditional platform buildings, on either side of the track, were reached from the flight of steps directly off Morningside Road. The booking hall, straddling the track, survives to the present day.
Crown copyright: RCAHMS ref. ED/13381.

1. Suburban railway
2. Morningside Cemetery
3. Morningside Road
4. Braid Church
5. Comiston Road
6. Former South Morningside Church
7. Cluny Parish Church
8. Hermitage Gardens

1. Four Ways
2. Edinburgh bypass
3. Inglis
4. Woodhall Nurseries
5. Torduff

Juniper Green, 1991

The picture is bisected by the City bypass running from left to right under Lanark Road. The road junction near the top of the picture is Four Ways where Lanark Road meets Gillespie Road and Hailes Road. Below the line of the bypass is the industrial complex of Alexander Inglis & Son Ltd, Grain Merchants, whose Head Office was transferred to Ormiston in 1997. The firm was established by Alexander Inglis at Juniper Green in 1910 and remained in the Inglis family until 1976. Various properties lie between Inglis' and Lanark Road including the glasshouses of the former Woodhall Nurseries (now demolished and replaced by housing), and Torduff (set back from the road) which was renamed Lorimer House after its architect, Robert S. Lorimer. The Water of Leith is hidden by the belt of trees to the right of Inglis' but part of the walkway, built on the track bed of the former Caledonian railway line to Balerno, can be seen to the left of the complex. At one time, the railway (opened in 1874) served stations at Colinton, Juniper Green, Currie and Balerno but passenger services were discontinued in 1943. Goods trains continued to serve the various mills along the valley until the 1960s when the line was closed and the track lifted. Although the mills were operating from at least the sixteenth century, Juniper Green did not develop as a distinct community until very much later. *Adair's Map* of 1735 shows the line of what is now Lanark Road passing through Curriemuir but the only places of habitation shown are Baberton to the north and Woodhall to the south. It was not until well into the nineteenth century that the village took on anything like its present-day layout. After Edinburgh was extended in 1920 to include Juniper Green, extensive bungalow development took place on the north side of the village.

Masons, with caps, pipes and aprons, employed on building villas at Curriemuirend, *c.* 1902.
Courtesy of the author.

Greenbank, 1991

Most of the district of Greenbank, lying between Braidburn Valley Park and the City Hospital, was built by Hepburn Brothers Ltd, Robinson the Builder, and Simon Keppie & Son between 1930 and 1940 on land which had previously been part of Greenbank Farm. The farmhouse and steadings stood near the east corner of Greenbank Gardens and Greenbank Loan. The north end of Greenbank Crescent was first developed from around 1908 but it was not until the 1930s that most of the fields of Greenbank Farm were built on. By far the largest number of houses were constructed by Hepburn Brothers Ltd, who were based in Dunfermline, each of the four brothers, Lawrence, James, Alexander and John, taking responsibility for separate parts of the business. Other family businesses involved in the building of Greenbank bungalows included: Richard Robinson, originally from County Tyrone,

and his son Richard J. Robinson; Simon Keppie & Son who were also established builders in Edinburgh; and Theodore K. Irvine originally from Lerwick who was also Provost of Bathgate from 1937 until his death in 1939. The bottom right-hand corner of the picture shows the former Greenlea Old People's Home (originally the City Poorhouse and now the Steils) under redevelopment, the Ambulance Depot, and the smoking chimney of the City Hospital. By 2000 most of the wards and departments at the City Hospital had been relocated and redevelopment of the hospital buildings and grounds into housing was well advanced. In the top right-hand corner of the picture is the collecting cistern for the outflow of water from the Hare, Fox, Swan and Peewit springs. Edinburgh's original water supply was first brought from the springs at Comiston in 1672.

The cover of Hepburn's brochure which advertised four-apartment bungalows for sale from £650 in the mid-1930s.
Courtesy of the author.

1. Collecting cistern
2. Greenbank Crescent
3. Greenbank Road
4. City Hospital
5. Site of Greenbank Farmhouse
6. Ambulance Depot
7. Greenlea, now the Steils

East

Crown copyright: RCAHMS ref: ED/11610/CN.

The late fifteenth-century Craigmillar Castle still retains its picturesque rural setting despite its proximity to the city. Adjacent is the Mains of Craigmillar, with Craigmillar Castle Road between it and Hawkhill Wood. Photographed in 1978.

CHAPTER 5

Craigmillar and Duddingston Breweries, 1930

The Craigmillar and Duddingston breweries were established between 1886 and 1902 on what was then a greenfield site, with a good supply of water, plenty space for expansion and, perhaps most importantly of all, excellent transport facilities to bring in the raw materials and take away the finished products. The opening of the Edinburgh Suburban and South Side Junction Railway in 1885 was undoubtedly one of the main features in establishing a brewing industry at Craigmillar. Sadly, the last working brewery, Drybrough & Co. Ltd, closed in 1987. At the present day all the brewery buildings in the picture have been demolished except Drybrough's which awaits imminent redevelopment in 2003.

The suburban line curves across the centre of the picture from left to right. Craigmillar Road (now Duddingston Road North) runs from the bottom left-hand corner, crosses over the suburban line, and continues on to the crossroads in the top right-hand corner. Straight ahead at the junction is Craigmillar Castle Road; Niddrie Mains Road is to the left (out of town); and Peffermill Road is to the right (into town). At these crossroads, two of the diagonal corners are built up: on the left is Cairntows Farm steading; and on the right is housing and Bristo Memorial Church, opened in 1904.

Prestonfield Golf Course is along the bottom edge of the picture. To the left of the green is Forkenford Farm steading, and to the left again, the St Leonard's branch line of the London & North Eastern Railway. The original track, designed by James Jardine, was opened in 1831 and was nicknamed the Innocent Railway, allegedly on account of its accident-free record.

There are four breweries to the right of Craigmillar Road: above the line of the suburban railway is Drybrough's Craigmillar Brewery (left) and Wm. Murray & Co. Ltd, North British Brewery (right). Below the line of the railway is the extensive Duddingston New Brewery, Robert Deuchar Ltd, whose name can be seen on the roof. Brewery House stands immediately to the right of the Innocent Railway where it crosses Craigmillar Road. The House is part of the adjacent Pentland Brewery, run by T. Y. Paterson & Co. Ltd.

There are also several brewing premises to the left of Craigmillar Road: the Raeburn Brewery, Robert Younger Ltd, is at the top of the picture, entered from Niddrie Mains Road; between the Raeburn Brewery and the tenement in the centre of the picture (Station Road, now Peffer Street) is the Castle Brewery of G. & J. Maclachlan Ltd; and to the left of the tenement, Craigmillar No. 1 Brewery, belonging to Wm. Murray & Co. Ltd. To the left of Murray's is Wm. McEwan's Craigmillar Maltings, and to the left again, the Brewers Food Supply Co. Ltd.

Crossroads at Craigmillar, c. 1932, looking north into Craigmillar Road, now Duddingston Road North. Cairntows Farmhouse is on the right, behind which is the stack for Maclachlan's Castle Brewery.
Courtesy of the author.

1. Raeburn Brewery, Younger
2. Cairntows Farm steading
3. Bristo Memorial Church
4. Castle Brewery, Maclachlan
5. Craigmillar Road
   (now Duddingston Road North)
6. Brewers Food Supply Co. Ltd
7. Craigmillar Maltings, McEwan
8. Craigmillar No. 1 Brewery, Murray
9. Craigmillar Brewery, Drybrough
10. North British Brewery, Murray
11. Duddingston Station and
    suburban railway
12. Duddingston New Brewery,
    Deuchar
13. Duddingston New Brewery,
    Deuchar
14. Brewery House
15. Pentland Brewery, Paterson
16. Innocent Railway
17. Forkenford Farm steading
18. Prestonfield Golf Course

1. Towerbank School
2. Brighton Mansions
3. Windsor Mansions
4. Marlborough Mansions
5. Straiton Place
6. Seabeach House
7. Bungalow Electric Theatre
8. Pavilion
9. Bath Street
10. Regent Street
11. Wellington Street (renamed Marlborough Street)

Bath Street, Portobello, 1930

Running northwards towards crowded beaches are (from left to right) Bath Street, Regent Street and Wellington Street, which was renamed Marlborough Street in 1968. Straiton Place runs from left to right, parallel to the Promenade. When this photograph was taken, Portobello was in its heyday as a seaside resort.

Bath Street dates from about 1801 and was the first street to be laid out north of Portobello High Street. By 1930 some of the original houses had been altered by the addition of shops built in the front garden ground. At the north end of the street there are handsome tenement blocks, two by the architect, Edward Calvert: on the left is Brighton Mansions with a date plaque, 1895, and on the right is Windsor Mansions, in Straiton Place, with a similar plaque on the face of the building with the date 1896. Marlborough Mansions, between Windsor Mansions and the beach, were demolished in 1971. As Portobello developed its reputation as a seaside resort, several places of entertainment grew up. In the bottom left-hand corner of the picture, the tent-like roof belongs to the Pavilion, known to the local children of the day as 'The Ghost House' where a number of challenging entertainments were available. By 1938 the site had been redeveloped as the County Cinema, designed by T. Bowhill Gibson. It was renamed the George in 1954 and closed in 1974. At the present day it is run as Royal George Bingo. Also showing in the picture, at No. 26 Bath Street, is the roof and cupola of the Bungalow Electric Theatre which later became a cinema and changed its name to the Victory, but closed in 1956. At the present day the building survives, minus the cupola, but the entire site is scheduled for redevelopment.

Regent Street and Wellington Street (now Marlborough Street) were laid out slightly later than Bath Street, by the architect, Lewis A. Wallace, from 1815, and have been subject to fewer alterations. Regent Street Church is at No. 21 and Portobello Congregational Church is in Wellington Street. Towerbank Primary School is in the top left-hand corner of the picture, built in 1885 and extended by the School Board architect, J. A Carfrae, in 1906. On the north side of Straiton Place, the interesting collection of buildings to the right of Windsor Mansions and Marlborough Mansions was demolished some years ago and replaced by a small play area for children. The very last house shown on the right-hand side is Seabeach House, now used as Seabeach Nursery.

Portobello Pier, by Thomas Bouch who also designed the ill-fated Tay Bridge, was opened near Marlborough Mansions in 1871 and demolished in 1917 before this photograph was taken.

A busy scene in Bath Street looking north towards the shore with Windsor Mansions at the far end of the street, c. 1907.
Courtesy of the author.

Portobello, 1941

The picture, taken on Monday, 19 May 1941, shows Portobello, looking north over the Firth of Forth, from above Portobello Public Park. The tall stack in the centre is Portobello Power Station which was demolished in 1978.

In 1891 Edinburgh Corporation was granted statutory powers to generate and distribute electricity throughout the city. The first power station was in Dewar Place, off Morrison Street, which began operating on 11 April 1895, with a direct current system for the city centre and an alternating current system for the suburbs. Despite a second power station coming into operation at McDonald Road in 1899, a report dated 1913 warned the Corporation that the city's two power stations were nearing their capacity. An eight-acre site for a much larger station was bought at Portobello, along with an extra twenty-four acres to the west of Baileyfield Road for railway sidings and coal storage. The Portobello site was ideal for a plentiful supply of water from the Forth for cooling, and good railway links to the Lothian coal mines. No progress was made with construction during the First World War but in 1922 a decision was taken to include East Lothian and Midlothian in the supply area. The first section of the power station was opened on 11 July 1923 by King George V. When the second section

was opened on 30 April 1930, increasing capacity to 116,500 kilowatts, Portobello was the first to supply the newly introduced national grid. The third section was opened on 12 April 1939 bringing the capacity up to 146,500 kilowatts.

At the bottom of the photograph, the large area of open ground is Portobello Public Park, to the left of which is Park Avenue and Duddingston Park, including Clifton Terrace. The smaller area of open ground in the right-hand corner is Duddingston Mains. Between the Park and Portobello Power Station are numerous railway tracks serving the main line, Portobello Goods Station and various sidings.

Right. Portobello Power Station, on the corner of King's Road and Portobello High Street, was opened on 11 July 1923 and demolished from 1978. From Edinburgh Corporation Electricity Supply, *1939.*

Below. The sidings and coal store were located to the west of Baileyfield Road. Wagons entered the rotary coal-tipping plant which inverted them, allowing the coal to fall into a giant hopper below the level of the track. The hopper then fed two conveyors which carried the coal into the power station. From Edinburgh Corporation Electricity Supply, *1939.*

1. Seafield Road
2. Portobello Power Station
3. Sidings
4. Portobello Public Park
5. Mainline and sidings
6. Duddingston Mains

1. Niddrie Pit bing
2. Niddrie Brick Works
3. Milton Road
4. Niddrie Cottages
5. Newcraighall Road
6. Klondyke Pit bing
7. Milton Road East
8. Pit baths
9. Klondyke Pit head
10. Brunstane
11. Newcraighall village

Newcraighall, 1946

The best point of reference between the 1946 photograph, opposite, and the 1991 photograph below is the distinctive bend in Newcraighall Road beside Niddrie Cottages. To the left of the bend is Niddrie Brick Works (now the site of Edinburgh Fort Retail Park) and further left again are the coal bings from the Niddrie pits. An even bigger bing (the site of which is now occupied by Kinnaird Park) lies to the right of the straight section of Newcraighall Road as it approaches the village of Newcraighall. This larger bing was created from the spoil taken from the famous Klondyke Pit which for many years employed most of the male population of the village until the pit closed in 1968. The rows of miners' cottages can be seen in the angle formed by the railway lines near the bottom edge of the picture. The village of Newcraighall was the setting for Bill Douglas' famous film trilogy, *My Childhood* in 1972, followed by *My Ain Folk* in 1973, and finally *My Way Home* in 1978, depicting his traumatic upbringing in Newcraighall which he conceded was not necessarily typical of life in a mining community.

Milton Road East, leading into Milton Road, is on the extreme right-hand side of the photograph. Midway between Newcraighall village and Milton Road East is the sixteenth-century farm and house of Brunstane. The original house belonged to the Crichtons of Brunstane. In the first half of the seventeenth century it was remodelled by Lord Maitland, and in 1672 a major extension was designed by Sir William Bruce. Later work was also executed by William Adam for Lord Milton who had bought the house in 1733.

Left. Niddrie Cottages, photographed in 1996, were built in Newcraighall Road *c.* 1880 with bricks from Niddrie Brickworks nearby. They have stood the test of time and, unlike many other buildings in the district, have survived the extensive redevelopment of the 1990s.
Crown copyright: RCAHMS ref. D/2338.

Left. In 1991, about the only points of reference remaining between the two aerial photographs are the distinctive bend in Newcraighall Road, and Niddrie Cottages, both of which have survived the huge building programme. The centre of the picture is occupied by the light-coloured roofs of the many retail outlets at Kinnaird Park. The A1 crosses over the bottom right-hand corner of the picture.
Crown copyright: RCAHMS ref. B/71060.

Klondyke Pit, Newcraighall, 1951

This picture, taken in a north-westerly direction, shows the pit-head buildings, the winding gear and the stack of the Klondyke Pit on the north side of Newcraighall Road. On the opposite side of the road (nearer to the camera), the long low building, with the tower at the right-hand end, is the pit baths. The light bridge across the road between the pit and the baths can just be seen in the picture. When this photograph was taken on Friday, 7 December 1951 several steam engines were working in and around the marshalling yards at Niddrie West Junction where various lines met.

Land at Newcraighall was acquired by the Niddrie Colliery Company in 1874 and by Benhar Colliery Company in 1876 although it is known that coalmining had been operational in the district for many years prior to that. In 1910 a vertical shaft was sunk, sixteen feet in diameter and almost 1000 feet in depth. In the 1920s production ran at over 250,000 tons per year, with more than a 1000 men employed producing coal for domestic and industrial use, and for export. From the bottom of the vertical shaft, roads were pushed further and further out. Those driven towards Fisherrow Harbour were known as the sea dooks and went under the Firth of Forth for a distance of over two miles from the Newcraighall shaft. When the coal industry was nationalised in 1947, the Niddrie &

Benhar pit was officially named Newcraighall, but it continued to be known locally as the Klondyke. After it was closed in 1968, due partly to geological problems, the pit buildings were all demolished and in 1971 the winding gear was dismantled and re-erected at Prestongrange Mining Museum.

Above. The Balfour Fountain, in the village of Newcraighall, was erected in June 1907 to the memory of Dr Andrew Balfour who for thirty years took a great interest in the health and well-being of the people of Newcraighall and its surroundings.
Photograph by the late A. C. Robson.

Left. Newcraighall Mine Rescue Team, winners of the First Cup, National Coal Board Area Competition, 1950.
Courtesy of J. McFarlane.

1. Niddrie West Junction
2. Niddrie Cottages
3. Newcraighall Road
4. Klondyke Pit bing
5. Klondyke Pit-head
6. Pit baths
7. Methodist Church
8. London & North Eastern Railway

1. Seafield Road
2. Former Marine Gardens
3. Former sports arena
4. Portobello Road
5. King's Road
6. Portobello Power Station
7. Portobello Open Air Pool
8. Figgate Burn
9. Fairground
10. Coal store
11. Baileyfield Road
12. Fishwives Causeway
13. Portobello High Street

Marine Gardens, Portobello, 1961

This vertical view of Portobello shows the intersection of Portobello Road, Seafield Road, King's Road, Portobello High Street and Baileyfield Road in the upper half of the picture. The former Marine Gardens sports centre and ballroom lies within the angle formed by Seafield Road and King's Road.

The Scottish National Exhibition was held at Saughton Hall in the summer of 1908. After the exhibition closed, a group of Edinburgh businessmen had the idea of buying up many of the temporary buildings and side-shows with a view to using them for a permanent entertainment park somewhere in Edinburgh. During the latter part of 1908 several possible areas were considered before the Portobello site was opened on 31 May 1909 by the Lord Provost of Edinburgh, Sir J. P. Gibson, in the company of the Provosts of Leith and Musselburgh. Unfortunately, much of the initial layout was radically altered, and the attractions closed to the public, at the outbreak of the First World War in 1914. During the war years, temporary Nissen huts were erected to house troops. At various times in its history, Marine Gardens has been home to a wide variety of interests. When it was first opened it took the name Edinburgh Marine Gardens and Zoological Park but it would appear that the menagerie did not remain open for long. There were balloon ascents, parachute jumps (sometimes into the sea!) and dare-devil jumps into water tanks. The sports stadium (the oval-shaped outline still visible in this 1961 photograph) was nearer to King's Road. It had a football pitch which was an early home ground of Leith Athletic Football Club, an athletics track, and latterly a dog-racing circuit and speedway track. In the 1960s, part of the site was used by Scottish Omnibuses but the last part of the ballroom building was not demolished until 1966.

Also showing in the picture is Portobello Power Station in the angle between King's Road and Portobello High Street. The adjacent light-coloured rectangle is Portobello Open Air Swimming Pool, opened in 1936 and unfortunately closed in 1980. When it was first opened it had a number of innovative features including artificial waves which could be activated after due warning to the bathers, and water partially heated from the adjacent power station. The large black area to the left of Baileyfield Road is the coal store and tipping plant (referred to on page 138) for Portobello Power Station.

Marine Gardens opened at Portobello in 1909 and provided a variety of entertainment, including ballroom dancing and roller skating.
Courtesy of the author.

Meadowbank Sports Centre and Restalrig, 1991

The photograph shows, from left to right, St Margaret's Railway Depot, Clockmill Lane, Old Meadowbank and New Meadowbank in 1951. Old Meadowbank was the home of Leith Athletic Football Club, and was surrounded by a speedway track, the home of the Edinburgh Monarchs. New Meadowbank consisted of a football pitch surrounded by an ash athletics track. The small white building, between the two tracks, was used as changing rooms and a house for the park supervisor.

Crown copyright: MoD ref. 540/RAF/501, SFFO, 0252.

Meadowbank Sports Centre and Velodrome appear in the bottom right-hand corner of the picture, separated from the houses of Marionville Park and Avenue by the Abbeyhill – Piershill railway loop. The Sports Centre was built in 1969 to designs by the City Architect's Department, at a cost of £2.5m, and was opened on 2 May 1970 by HRH The Duke of Kent in time for the XI Commonwealth Games held at Meadowbank from 16-25 July. The complex was built on the site of a fairly rudimentary cinder athletics track and a separate speedway stadium. The Velodrome was also built in 1969 for the Commonwealth Games, but was dismantled in 1985 and renewed in time for the 1986 Commonwealth Games at which every cycle record was broken by the Australian team. The track, 24 feet wide (7.3 metres), is made of West African hardwood and allows a safe riding maximum speed of 90 kilometres per hour. Over the years, Meadowbank has attracted several national and international conferences and sporting events, notably the Europa Cup 1973, but it is primarily a centre of sport and leisure for the local community. Over 12,000 people use the facilities each week to play, or be coached in, all the major games and sports.

The old village of Restalrig lies to the left of the Velodrome, between Marionville Drive and Restalrig Road South. St Margaret's Parish Church, previously Restalrig, lies in the centre of the village. There has been some form of ecclesiastical presence here since the twelfth century, which reached its height in the fifteenth century before being eclipsed at the Reformation in 1560. Adjacent to the church is the famous St Triduana's Well, named after St Triduana, who, according to legend, came to Restalrig where she spent her days healing and comforting the blind.

Almost in the centre of the picture, to the right of the traffic roundabout, is St Ninian's Roman Catholic Church, designed by Giles Gilbert Scott in 1929. The adjacent, eighteenth-century Marionville House, formerly the property of the church, was the home of the infamous Captain Macrae around 1790. He died in obscurity on 16 January 1820 having had to flee the country after killing his friend, Sir George Ramsay, in a duel, called as a result of the two men arguing over whose member of staff ordered a sedan chair outside the Old Theatre Royal at the East End of Princes Street.

In the upper part of the picture Craigentinny House, the sixteenth-century home of the Nisbets of Dean, now a Community Centre, is on the left-hand side of Loaning Road, and Craigentinny Primary School, opened in 1935, is in Loganlea Drive.

1. Craigentinny School
2. Craigentinny House
3. Restalrig Road South
4. St Margaret's (previously Restalrig)
   and St Triduana's Well
5. Marionville House
6. Marionville Avenue
7. Velodrome
8. St Ninian's RC Church
9. Abbeyhill – Piershill railway loop
10. Marionville Park
11. Meadowbank Sports Centre

Crown copyright: RCAHMS ref: C/40286 CN.

CHAPTER 6

West

An autumn scene to the west of the City bypass, looking towards Sighthill and Wester Hailes. The fields in the foreground are traversed, from left to right, by the M8 extension in the course of construction, the Union Canal, and the A70 road to the Calders. Photographed in 1994.

Longstone and Slateford, 1930

This view of Slateford, looking south, gives an excellent idea of how the roads, the canal and the railway have, over the years, spanned the valley of the Water of Leith. The old road to Lanark crosses the picture from left to right and joins Inglis Green Road which leads to Longstone. For many years the villages of Slateford and Longstone were quite separate, but building development after the Second World War soon filled the vacant ground. The canal aqueduct and the railway viaduct run parallel to one another to the north of Slateford's main street. The Union Canal, begun in 1818, was built from Port Hopetoun in Fountainbridge to join the Forth and Clyde Canal at Falkirk, a distance of thirty-one miles, and cost nearly half a million pounds, or almost twice the original estimate, in 1813. The aqueduct carries the canal across the valley on eight arches, to the north of which is the much lower, fourteen-arch railway viaduct built in 1847. When this photograph was taken, the track was owned by the London Midland Scottish Railway which also laid sidings to serve the Gorgie cattle markets and A. & J. Macnab, Cleaners and Dyers to the north of the viaduct.

The large industrial complex in the centre of the picture is occupied by A. & J. Macnab. The ground was first used in 1773 as a bleachfield by Joseph Reid whose ailing business was taken over by Hugh McWhirter a few years later. The McWhirters were followed by the Macnabs in 1849 and the Stevensons

in 1899 who retained the name. Macnab's workers' cottages can be seen on both sides of Inglis Green Road near the viaduct, and the two large houses in the private grounds to the right were owned by the Stevenson family.

On the extreme left, beside the hay-stacks, are the cattle markets and slaughterhouses relocated to Gorgie from Fountainbridge in 1902, and in the top left-hand corner the open field is now occupied by the bungalows of Allan Park. At the bottom of the picture, lying in the angle formed by Inglis Green Road and the Water of Leith, is the seventeenth-century Gray's Mill, demolished in 1988. It was here that Bonnie Prince Charlie was based whilst he negotiated the surrender of Edinburgh in 1745. A plaque commemorating the event is fixed to the underside of the arch of the concrete bridge which carries the Union Canal over Slateford Road at the foot of Craiglockhart Avenue.

Right. In the foreground are the workers' cottages in Inglis Green Road. The large complex behind is the cleaning and dyeing plant of A. & J. Macnab, c. 1910.
Courtesy of the author.

Right. Inglis Green Road looking south to the railway and canal bridges where the road is narrow enough to use only one of the arches of the viaduct. On the right of the picture is the entrance and lodge house to the much grander properties owned by the Stevenson family, proprietors of A. & J. Macnab, c. 1908.
Courtesy of the author.

1. Gorgie slaughter houses
2. Aqueduct
3. Lanark Road
4. Viaduct
5. A. & J. Macnab
6. Workers' cottages
7. Stevenson's house
8. Stevenson's house
9. Water of Leith
10. Inglis Green Road
11. Saughton Cemetery
12. Gray's Mill

18790

18790

1. Saughton Mansion
2. Shandon
3. Caledonian Railway
4. Meggetland
5. 1937 bridge
6. Allan Park
7. Macandrew's bridge
8. Union Canal
9. Craiglockhart Church
10. Craiglockhart Road North

Slateford and Craiglockhart, 1943

When this photograph was taken on the afternoon of Friday, 22 October 1943 the country was in the grip of the Second World War but, from the air, there is no evidence of the hostilities. Slateford and Craiglockhart are in the foreground and Gorgie and Shandon are in the background.

The dark line of the Union Canal snakes across the picture from the bottom left-hand corner. The canal narrows as it is carried across the Slateford aqueduct and then curves sharply to the right as it crosses over Slateford Road at the foot of Craiglockhart Avenue. The very distinctive white concrete bridge had been in existence for only a few years when this photograph was taken, having replaced the original, much narrower, bridge in 1937. The canal then runs between the districts of Allan Park and Craiglockhart, and on to Meggetland playing fields. Just before it reaches Meggetland there is a small pedestrian bridge over the canal. This was built in the first decade of the twentieth century to carry a light railway from Slateford to Redford Barracks. The railway was used to carry the vast quantities of stone and timber needed for the construction of the Barracks between 1909 and 1915. The line of the railway was still evident in Craiglockhart Road North when nearby houses were being built in 1923. Although most of Craiglockhart is built up in the picture, there are still one or two vacant feus, notably on the north corner of Craiglockhart Road North and Craiglockhart Avenue. Another more detailed photograph of Craiglockhart in 1930 appears on page 111.

The line of the Caledonian Railway runs parallel to the canal as they pass through Slateford but thereafter the Railway maintains a straight line as far as Shandon before veering to the left as it proceeds to Princes Street Station. Further afield, in the top left-hand corner of the photograph, is Saughton Hall Mansion near Balgreen Road, details of which are given at page 161.

Left. Electric tram, service No. 4 in 1946 at the terminus in Slateford Road, a few yards east of the junction with Chesser Avenue. The tram is a Standard model built at Shrubhill, Leith Walk. *Courtesy of the author.*

Below. The entrance gates to what is now Saughton Park were erected in 1908 as the principal gateway to the Scottish National Exhibition, held in the grounds of Saughton Hall Mansion which can be seen in the background, c. 1912. *Courtesy of the author.*

Corstorphine Village, 1942

Many of Edinburgh's present-day suburbs, such as Colinton, Juniper Green and Corstorphine, were separate villages up until 1920 and did not come within the city boundary. That separate identity was still evident when this photograph of Corstorphine was taken on Friday, 8 May 1942. Although bungalow development in the 1930s has greatly extended the old village, Corstorphine is still shown as quite separate from the remainder of the city and is almost completely surrounded by open farmland.

The photograph is taken in a north-westerly direction, the stone piers of the Forth Railway Bridge just visible in the centre of the top edge of the picture. There are three railway lines visible, belonging to the London and North Eastern Railway. The main line running west from Haymarket divides at Balgreen (off the right-hand edge of the picture) to provide a local service to Pinkhill Station and Corstorphine Station which was the end of the line. Further west (in the bottom left-hand corner of the picture) the main line divides again: straight ahead is the Glasgow line; and curving sharply to the right at Carrick Knowe is the line to Fife and the north of Scotland. The track can be seen in the open countryside all the way to the Forth Railway Bridge, hidden for a short distance only by low-level cloud above the Maybury road junction. Two arterial roads out of Edinburgh are also visible: running through the built up area is St John's Road leading onto Corstorphine Road; and in the top right-hand corner of the picture, Queensferry Road has ribbon development mostly on its south side. Running between the two arterial roads, Maybury Road, Drum Brae and Clermiston Road, have long sections with open fields on both sides.

In the bottom right-hand corner is Carricknowe Golf Course, normally laid out with tees, bunkers and greens. The double lines of geometric formation are, however, holes dug in the fairways, which probably had poles inserted, to prevent enemy aircraft from landing.

Right. Girls at the maypole in the playground of Corstorphine Primary School. In 1996 the school held a celebration to mark 350 years of education in the old village, c. 1908.
Courtesy of the author.

Below. Looking east (towards the city centre) on the High Street of Corstorphine Village. The low cottages facing down the High Street are part of Irish Corner, long since demolished, and the ornamental gate pillars on the right lead to the Dower House. Irish Corner was named from the Irish workers who lived there whilst employed on the construction of the Union Canal and the railways, c. 1912.
Courtesy of the author.

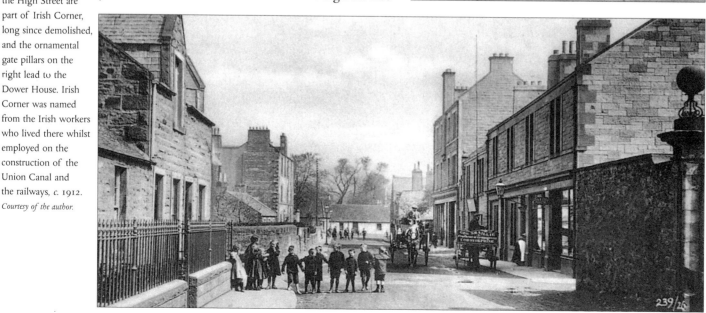

1. Forth Railway Bridge
2. Maybury Junction
3. Maybury Road
4. Drum Brae
5. Queensferry Road
6. Aberdeen railway line
7. St John's Road
8. Clermiston Road
9. Glasgow railway
10. Carrick Knowe
11. Corstorphine Station
12. Carricknowe Golf Course

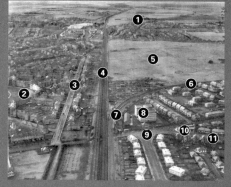

1. Aberdeen railway line
2. Whitson Crescent
3. Whitson Road
4. Glasgow and Aberdeen railway line
5. Carricknowe Golf Course
6. Corstorphine railway line
7. Balgreen Halt
8. Jenner's Depository
9. Balgreen Road
10. St Cuthbert's Co-operative
11. Saughtonhall Drive

Balgreen, 1951

The railway line, running vertically in the centre of the picture, is the combined Edinburgh to Glasgow and Edinburgh to Aberdeen route as it passes Balgreen. Two lines strike off to the right: one in the foreground and one in the background. The one in the foreground, going to Corstorphine, was opened in 1902 and was already in operation when Balgreen Halt was opened temporarily to serve people attending the Scottish National Exhibition at Saughtonhall in 1908. Balgreen Halt was not opened on a permanent basis until 1934. The Corstorphine line was closed in 1967. The line in the background of the picture curves to the right at Carrick Knowe, en route for the Forth Bridge and Aberdeen.

By far the largest building is the distinctive red brick Jenners Depository in Balgreen Road by the architect, James B. Dunn. In April 1926 Jenners applied to the Dean of Guild Court for permission 'to erect a Depository, Motor Garage, Entrance Lodge, Unclimbable surrounding fence etc., at Balgreen Road, Murrayfield'. A copy of the plans had to be deposited with the London and North Eastern Railway Company of Waterloo Place in Edinburgh as owners of the adjacent land. The proposed building consisted of two five-storey blocks connected by a smaller central section containing the lift, stairwell and offices, all with concrete floors and fireproof doors. Permission to build was granted subject to minor alterations and building work started shortly thereafter. Its initial use was to store the furniture and effects of Edinburgh residents working abroad, but since 1980 it has been used for storing Jenners' own retail stock. The 1926 plans also allowed for fairly substantial lodges, one on either side of the entrance gates, consisting of a living room, three bedrooms, bathroom and scullery with larder and coal cellar.

Balgreen Halt lies to the left of the Depository where the Corstorphine line meets the main track. To the left of the main track, and running parallel to it, is Whitson Road and Crescent leading into the district of Stenhouse. St Cuthbert's Co-operative has a long frontage, beside the police-box, on the corner of Balgreen Road and Saughtonhall Drive. The shop included a grocer, baker, butcher and fruiterer.

Balgreen Halt was about a mile west of Haymarket where the Corstorphine branch line left the main line. On the left of the picture, two preserved locomotives are pulling a special train, carrying members of the International Wrought Non Ferrous Metals Council returning to Edinburgh from an excursion to Pitlochry on 13 June 1963. The locomotives are an ex-Highland Railway 4-6-0 No. 103, and ex-Caledonian Railway 4-2-2 No. 123.
Photograph by G. M. Staddon.

Stenhouse, Carrick Knowe, Saughton Mains and Broomhouse, 1951

Continuing the railway theme westwards, the photograph shows the junction of the Glasgow line and the Aberdeen line with Saughton Road coming in from the left and running under the railway.

The prominent circle along the bottom edge of the photograph is Stenhouse Grove with Stenhouse Drive running through the centre of it. To the left of the Grove is the copper, cruciform-shaped roof of St Aidan's Church, designed by J. Inch Morrison in 1933 and built of red brick. When the congregation first moved to Stenhouse from Bread Street they worshipped in the hall until the main building was completed. St Aidan's was demolished c. 1997 after the union with Stenhouse Saughton in Gorgie Road. Two larger buildings lie to the left of St Aidan's. The first is the quadrangle of Saughton Junior Secondary School opened in September 1939 but temporarily closed, almost immediately, at the outbreak of the Second World War. It changed its name to Carrickvale in 1949 and was later used as Stevenson College Annexe before becoming a community centre. The building further to the left is Stenhouse Primary School, designed by the Edinburgh School Board architect, John A. Carfrae, in 1929. On the opposite side of Saughton Mains Street to Carrickvale School is St Salvador's Episcopal Church, designed by the architects, Tarbolton & Ochterlony. The foundation stone was laid on 11 December 1937 and the church was opened in November 1938, but the full plan was never implemented. The quadrangle of buildings to the left of St Salvador's is the steading of Saughton Mains Farm. The almost square area of ground between St Salvador's and the railway has numerous prefabs built at the end of the Second World War as temporary houses, but not demolished until 1965. The long low building standing on its own is Carrickvale School Annexe. The open area around it was used as the sports ground.

To the right of the railway track is Carrick Knowe, the first development of 856 houses being started in 1935. The builders, Mactaggart & Mickel, expended £1,600, on average, to erect a block of four three-apartment flats which were rented out at £27 per annum by the factors, Gumley & Davidson. To the west of North Saughton Road (i.e. further out of town) the light-coloured pavilions of the Government offices stand out against the darker construction of the houses of Broomhouse which are still being built. The 1946 Government building was originally designed as a convalescent hospital but was never used as such. Further west again is the beginning of Sighthill Industrial Estate.

Right. Carrickvale Secondary School 1st XI Hockey Team at the school in 1951.
Courtesy of Mrs Sheila Miller.

Below right. St Salvador's Church hall was built first and used for worship until the church was completed in 1938. The photograph shows the workmen laying out the foundations for the church building in 1937.
Courtesy of Mrs Sheila Miller and Joan Sutherland.

1. Sighthill Industrial Estate
2. Saughton Road North
3. Government offices
4. Carrick Knowe
5. Saughton Mains Farm steadings
6. St Salvador's Episcopal Church
7. Carrickvale School Annexe
8. Stenhouse School
9. Carrickvale School
10. St Aidan's Church
11. Stenhouse Drive

1. Saughton Prison
2. Greyhound stadium
3. Stenhouse Drive
4. Chesser Avenue
5. Saughton Hall
6. Saughton Enclosure
7. Balgreen Road
8. Lade
9. Gorgie Road
10. Cox's
11. Roxy Cinema
12. Westfield Court

Saughton Rose Garden and Public Park, 1951

Gorgie Road runs diagonally left from the bottom edge of the photograph to the junction with Balgreen Road on the right. The road then continues in a straight line to the junction with Stenhouse Drive, then swings to the right as it passes Saughton Prison.

In the foreground of the picture Cox's Glue Works is on the left of Gorgie Road beside the railway tracks which serve Gorgie slaughterhouses. The lade bringing water from the Water of Leith is just visible entering the works from the west. Westfield Court, in the course of construction, is in the bottom right-hand corner of the picture. Between it and Gorgie Road is Poole's Roxy Cinema which opened on 20 December 1937. The Poole family had been involved in the cinema business since the end of the nineteenth century, their first Edinburgh venture being Charles W. Poole's 'panoramic shows' at the Synod Hall in Castle Terrace. The Roxy was designed by Chadwick Watson & Company to seat 1,600 and was very successful for the following twenty years until the decline in cinema audiences in the late 1950s forced its closure in 1963.

Saughton Hall Mansion is in the centre of the picture surrounded by ornamental gardens. This photograph, taken on 18 May 1951, must be one of the last images of this great mansion as it was demolished in 1952. It was probably built by Robert Baird, the Edinburgh merchant, after he bought the estate in 1660. During the nineteenth century, the mansion was used as Saughton Hall Asylum 'for the reception of Patients of the higher rank', under the direction of Dr W. H. Lowe, followed by Dr John Barry Tuke. At the beginning of the twentieth century the grounds of Saughton Hall Mansion were used for the Scottish National Exhibition of 1908 which drew large crowds from Edinburgh and throughout Scotland, as well as many overseas visitors. Between 1 May and 31 October 1908 the total number of admissions was 3.5 million. Unfortunately, during the following decades the mansion was allowed to deteriorate badly as a result of which the owners, Edinburgh Corporation, felt they had no option but to demolish it. To the right of the mansion are sports fields and Saughton Enclosure.

Below left. This vertical picture, on 23 June 1961, is taken directly above Saughton Prison, to the left of which are allotment gardens, Saughton Cemetery and the oval track belonging to the Greyhound Racing Association. *Crown copyright: MoD ref. 58/RAF/4488.*

Below right. The Industrial Hall at the Scottish National Exhibition held in the grounds of Saughtonhall Mansion in the summer of 1908. *Courtesy of the author.*

Davidson's Mains and Hillpark, 1951

Queensferry Road runs vertically from the centre of the bottom edge of the picture. It curves gently to the left as it passes Quality Street, on the right, and Craigcrook Road on the left. Further out of town, Queensferry Road is seen to curve again to the right just before the junction with Drum Brae North.

Quality Street leads to the village of Davidson's Mains, or Muttonhole as it was first known. Several derivations of the name have been suggested, the most favoured being a haugh, or flat area of ground, where sheep were pastured. The origin of the name Davidson's Mains is much more definite: it comes from the Davidson family who owned the mansion of Muirhouse in Marine Drive. Davidson's Mains Railway Station is in the centre of the village on the London Midland Scottish branch line which terminated at Barnton. Passenger trains ceased to run in 1951 but goods trains used the line as far as Davidson's Mains goods yard for several years thereafter. Shortly after 1951 the railway bridge across Cramond Road South was removed to allow the use of double-decker buses. Davidson's Mains Primary School is on the left of Corbiehill Road in the bottom right-hand corner of the picture. It was built in 1874, enlarged in 1907, and demolished in 1967 when the present school was built on the adjacent site.

Part of Blackhall and Hillpark lie to the left of Queensferry Road. The bungalows of Blackhall were built in the late 1920s and early 1930s on the Craigcrook estate. In the photograph, the houses of Hillpark are still under construction: those nearest to Craigcrook Road are complete but, further up the hill, at Hillpark Avenue, there are several vacant feus. The estate was begun by Mactaggart & Mickel in 1936 who described the area in their sales brochure as 'Overlooking the beautiful woodlands of Davidson's Mains and Corstorphine Hill Parks – the finest residential district in Edinburgh, yet only 12 minutes from Princes Street'. Prices varied from £900 to £1,180 for

a five-apartment bungalow. Although many of the houses were provided with garages, the age of the motor car had obviously not fully arrived – the sales brochure advised prospective purchasers to travel to the estate by bus, or by train from the Caledonian Station (at the west end of Princes Street) to Davidson's Mains Station. The first house to be sold at Hillpark was No. 409 Queensferry Road, a six-apartment villa with a garage (in 1936 for £1,485). During the Second World War building work was severely restricted on account of a severe shortage of basic materials and also reluctance on the part of the public to make long-term commitments to house-buying, but after 1945 interest in the estate quickly returned.

A 1937 advertisement for houses at the Hillpark Estate built by Mactaggart & Mickel Ltd.

Mactaggart & Mickel Collection: RCAHMS.

HILLPARK ESTATE

OVERLOOKING THE BEAUTIFUL WOODLANDS OF DAVIDSON'S MAINS & CORSTORPHINE HILL PARKS. THE FINEST RESIDENTIAL DISTRICT IN EDINBURGH, YET ONLY 12 MINUTES FROM PRINCES STREET.

This picturesque estate in the Queensferry Road has been chosen as the site for a limited number of distinguished Bungalows and Villas. Each design has been prepared with due regard to the amenities of its setting and the architecture is dignified and practical. Every house has a charming aspect and many have an uninterrupted vista of magnificent parkland.

The above illustration shows a 5-apartment Bungalow for which the price is £1100. There are also other types of houses ranging in price from £900. Prices include road charges.

Show Houses are now open daily (including Sundays) from 1 p.m. until dusk and inspection is cordially invited.

HOW TO GET THERE. S.M.T. or Corporation 'Buses from Hope Street Post Office (West End) to Craigcrook Road or Davidson's Mains Cross respectively. Trains from Caledonian Station (L.M.S.) to Davidson's Mains.

Mactaggart & Mickel Ltd

67 YORK PLACE - - - - - - EDINBURGH
TELEPHONE — EDINBURGH 21717

1. Drum Brae North
2. Hillpark
3. Quality Street
4. Davidson's Mains
5. Barnton railway line
6. Craigcrook Road
7. Queensferry Road
8. Davidson's Mains School
9. Blackhall
10. Corbiehill Road

1. Kirkliston
2. Runway 13/31
3. Turnhouse Road
4. Main terminal
5. RAF married quarters
6. Runway 26/08
7. Control tower
8. C type hangar
9. RAF complex
10. Fuel depot
11. Fuel pumps
12. Edinburgh Flying Club
13. Aberdeen railway line
14. Maintenance
15. Garage for snow-clearing ploughs

Turnhouse, 1966

Turnhouse Airport in 1966 bears little resemblance to the present-day Edinburgh Airport owned and run by the British Airports Authority. The photograph is taken in a westerly direction above the Edinburgh to Aberdeen main line railway, looking towards Kirkliston, with the shale bings at Winchburgh in the far distance. The old road to Kirkliston (Turnhouse Road) crosses over the railway track just off the right-hand edge of the picture, and passes very close to the striped tarmac area denoting the end of the main 13/31 runway. The second runway, 26/08, crosses at right angles.

A number of ancillary buildings lie near the line of the railway at the bottom of the picture. From left to right they are: underground fuel tanks beside two adjacent Nissen huts; fuel pumps at the end of a short curved access road; the Edinburgh Flying Club at two Nissen huts at right angles to one another, with adjacent tennis courts; and two small groups of buildings, near the railway track, for ground maintenance staff.

The largest group of buildings is on the right-hand side of the picture adjacent to Turnhouse Road. The largest building, with the open frontage facing the camera, is a maintenance C type hangar. Between it and the railway, the low building with the double doors was used for garaging snow-clearing equipment. To the left of the C type hangar is the control tower and fire station, beyond which is the main terminal where the aircraft are waiting to taxi out to the runway. To the right of Turnhouse Road are buildings belonging to the RAF, including the Sergeants' married quarters, the mess, parade ground, Commander's residence and the Turnhouse Flying Club. In 1966, when the photograph was taken, it was still common practice to stop traffic temporarily on the Kirkliston road to allow aircraft to land. There were manual barriers across the road operated by two men stationed at small 'sentry' boxes. This section of the Kirkliston road was not closed until a new runway was built in the early 1970s.

Turnhouse Airport was first established in 1916, but in the early days there was not a lot of traffic. However, on 27 October 1938, No. 603 City of Edinburgh (Bomber) Squadron, Auxiliary Air Force, based at Turnhouse, was converted into the first Fighter Squadron in Scotland, and was involved in heroic air combat throughout the Second World War.

During the year ending 31 March 2002 Edinburgh Airport carried: 6,255,585 passengers; 15,509 metric tonnes of cargo; and 38,082 metric tonnes of mail.

The main terminal at Turnhouse Airport in the late 1950s, showing two McDonnell Douglas DC-3s, commonly known as 'Dakotas'. The DC-3 on the right is from Aer Lingus, a regular user of Turnhouse Airport. A total of 13,641 Dakotas were built by the Douglas Aircraft Company, Santa Monica, California from 1935 to the late 1940s.
Courtesy of the author.

Baberton Mains and Wester Hailes, 1991

The large group of houses in the centre of the picture, arranged around an area of open space, is Baberton Mains, built by Wimpey, the house builder, in the 1970s. Most of the streets of Baberton Mains are built on the fields of Fernieflat, the Gardens being laid out on the site of Fernieflat farmhouse and steading.

Part of Baberton Golf Course appears in the bottom right-hand corner of the picture. The original nine-hole course, designed by Willie Park, was opened on 15 July 1893 but within a very short time it was extended to eighteen holes. Membership was initially restricted to residents of the parish of Colinton and Currie but that requirement has long since been abandoned.

Juniper Green Primary School is also on the extreme right of the picture. The first Juniper Green school was the Female Subscription School, the second was the 1910 building on the corner of Baberton Avenue and Woodhall Terrace, and the third one is the building seen here.

At the top of the picture is the long sweeping curve of the City bypass, running under Lanark Road. The former Juniper Green Bowling Green was removed when the bypass was built. The Club was relocated nearer to the centre of the village. Four Ways, the junction of Gillespie Road, Lanark Road and Wester Hailes Road, is at the top edge of the photograph. Wester Hailes Road leads down to Clovenstone Roundabout, giving access to the houses of Wester Hailes, many of which were built in the late 1960s and early 1970s. The site of the house and steading of Wester Hailes is now occupied by the Green Way through the district. Wester Hailes Road follows substantially the line of what was known as Thieves Road, running between Calder Road and Lanark Road. Fortunately, there is no need for the residents of any of the neighbouring districts to be concerned. Stuart Harris in *The Place Names of Edinburgh* states that the name is more likely to be based on the early Scots *theve*, meaning a hawthorn or bramble growing along the hedgerows.

The name Fernieflat dates from at least the middle of the eighteenth century. This handsome farmhouse with the twin crow-stepped gables, and the steadings behind, were all swept away for the construction of Baberton Mains Gardens in the early 1970s, *c.* 1910. *Courtesy of the author.*

FERNIE FLAT JUNIPER GREEN

1. Four Ways
2. Clovenstone roundabout
3. City Bypass
4. Lanark Road
5. Juniper Green School
6. Baberton Mains Drive
7. Baberton Golf Course

Index

Entries in italics denote photographs or publications.